U.S. GROUND FORCES AND THE DEFENSE OF CENTRAL EUROPE

Studies in Defense Policy
TITLES IN PRINT

Support Costs in the Defense Budget: The Submerged One-Third
Martin Binkin

The Changing Soviet Navy
Barry M. Blechman

Strategic Forces: Issues for the Mid-Seventies
Alton H. Quanbeck and Barry M. Blechman

U.S. Reserve Forces: The Problem of the Weekend Warrior
Martin Binkin

U.S. Force Structure in NATO: An Alternative
Richard D. Lawrence and Jeffrey Record

U.S. Tactical Air Power: Missions, Forces, and Costs
William D. White

U.S. Nuclear Weapons in Europe: Issues and Alternatives
Jeffrey Record with the assistance of Thomas I. Anderson

The Control of Naval Armaments: Prospects and Possibilities
Barry M. Blechman

Stresses in U.S.-Japanese Security Relations
Fred Greene

The Military Pay Muddle
Martin Binkin

Sizing Up the Soviet Army
Jeffrey Record

Where Does the Marine Corps Go from Here?
Martin Binkin and Jeffrey Record

Deterrence and Defense in Korea: The Role of U.S. Forces
Ralph N. Clough

Women and the Military
Martin Binkin and Shirley J. Bach

The Soviet Military Buildup and U.S. Defense Spending
Barry M. Blechman and others

Soviet Air Power in Transition
Robert P. Berman

Shaping the Defense Civilian Work Force: Economics, Politics, and National Security
Martin Binkin with Herschel Kanter and Rolf H. Clark

The Military Equation in Northeast Asia
Stuart E. Johnson with Joseph A. Yager

Youth or Experience? Manning the Modern Military
Martin Binkin and Irene Kyriakopoulos

Paying the Modern Military
Martin Binkin and Irene Kyriakopoulos

Defense in the 1980s
William W. Kaufmann

The FX Decision: "Another Crucial Moment" in U.S.-China-Taiwan Relations
A. Doak Barnett

Planning Conventional Forces, 1950–80
William W. Kaufmann

Blacks and the Military
Martin Binkin and Mark J. Eitelberg with Alvin J. Schexnider and Marvin M. Smith

U.S. Arms Sales: The China-Taiwan Tangle
A. Doak Barnett

Soviet Strategic Forces: Requirements and Responses
Robert P. Berman and John C. Baker

U.S. Ground Forces and the Defense of Central Europe
William P. Mako

STUDIES IN DEFENSE POLICY

U.S. GROUND FORCES AND THE DEFENSE OF CENTRAL EUROPE

William P. Mako

THE BROOKINGS INSTITUTION
Washington, D.C.

Copyright © 1983 by
THE BROOKINGS INSTITUTION
1775 Massachusetts Avenue, N.W., Washington, D.C. 20036

Library of Congress Cataloging in Publication data:
Mako, William P., 1954–
 U.S. ground forces and the defense of Central Europe.
 (Studies in defense policy)
 Includes bibliographical references.
 1. North Atlantic Treaty Organization—Armed Forces.
2. North Atlantic Treaty Organization—United States.
3. Central Europe—Defenses. 4. Warsaw Treaty Organization—Armed Forces. I. Title. II. Title: US ground forces and the defense of Central Europe. III. Series.
UA 646.3.M243   1983   355′.031′091821   83-2817
ISBN 0-8157-5444-7
ISBN 0-8157-5443-4 (pbk.)

9 8 7 6 5 4 3 2 1

Board of Trustees
Robert V. Roosa
Chairman
Andrew Heiskell
Vice Chairman;
Chairman, Executive Committee
Louis W. Cabot
Vice Chairman
Vincent M. Barnett, Jr.
Barton M. Biggs
Frank T. Cary
A. W. Clausen
William T. Coleman, Jr.
Lloyd N. Cutler
Thomas Donahue
Charles W. Duncan, Jr.
George M. Elsey
Robert F. Erburu
Hanna H. Gray
Robert D. Haas
Philip M. Hawley
Roger W. Heyns
James T. Lynn
Bruce K. MacLaury
Robert S. McNamara
Arjay Miller
Herbert P. Patterson
Donald S. Perkins
J. Woodward Redmond
Charles W. Robinson
James D. Robinson III
Ralph S. Saul
Henry B. Schacht
Roger D. Semerad
Gerard C. Smith
Howard R. Swearer
Morris Tanenbaum
Phyllis A. Wallace

Honorary Trustees
Eugene R. Black
Robert D. Calkins
Edward W. Carter
Bruce B. Dayton
Douglas Dillon
Huntington Harris
John E. Lockwood
William McC. Martin, Jr.
H. Chapman Rose
Robert Brookings Smith
Sydney Stein, Jr.

THE BROOKINGS INSTITUTION is an independent organization devoted to nonpartisan research, education, and publication in economics, government, foreign policy, and the social sciences generally. Its principal purposes are to aid in the development of sound public policies and to promote public understanding of issues of national importance.

The Institution was founded on December 8, 1927, to merge the activities of the Institute for Government Research, founded in 1916, the Institute of Economics, founded in 1922, and the Robert Brookings Graduate School of Economics and Government, founded in 1924.

The Board of Trustees is responsible for the general administration of the Institution, while the immediate direction of the policies, program, and staff is vested in the President, assisted by an advisory committee of the officers and staff. The by-laws of the Institution state: "It is the function of the Trustees to make possible the conduct of scientific research, and publication, under the most favorable conditions, and to safeguard the independence of the research staff in the pursuit of their studies and in the publication of the results of such studies. It is not a part of their function to determine, control, or influence the conduct of particular investigations or the conclusions reached."

The President bears final responsibility for the decision to publish a manuscript as a Brookings book. In reaching his judgment on the competence, accuracy, and objectivity of each study, the President is advised by the director of the appropriate research program and weighs the views of a panel of expert outside readers who report to him in confidence on the quality of the work. Publication of a work signifies that it is deemed a competent treatment worthy of public consideration but does not imply endorsement of conclusions or recommendations.

The Institution maintains its position of neutrality on issues of public policy in order to safeguard the intellectual freedom of the staff. Hence interpretations or conclusions in Brookings publications should be understood to be solely those of the authors and should not be attributed to the Institution, to its trustees, officers, or other staff members, or to the organizations that support its research.

FOREWORD

WHETHER Western Europe could be defended without resort to nuclear weapons has been a driving military and political issue within the North Atlantic Treaty Organization for over three decades. The prevailing judgment among the Western allies has been pessimistic. With the capacity to mobilize up to 120 army divisions and several thousand attack aircraft, the Soviet Union and its Eastern European allies have been conceded a preponderance in conventional arms that could be offset, it is argued, only by nuclear weapons. NATO has acquired a nuclear arsenal to counter the threat from the east, withstanding in the process strenuous objections from those opposed to reliance on nuclear defense. Recent plans to equip the NATO forces with improved nuclear weapons have renewed controversy, inflamed political emotions, and redirected attention to the prior question of defense by conventional arms.

In this study William P. Mako reviews the history of NATO Conventional force preparations and discusses the assessments that various observers have made of NATO's capacity to resist an assault by the Eastern bloc. He discusses the assumptions and force-balance calculations on which such assessments rest. Avoiding complacent and alarmist extremes, he concludes that neither successful NATO defense nor successful Warsaw Pact aggression can be confidently predicted as the outcome of conventional warfare in Western Europe. At the moment deterrence rests on that mutual uncertainty. Aware that NATO's chances for success in conventional defense would be lessened if U.S. forces had to be diverted to another theater, he recommends a modest strengthening of U.S. and allied reserve forces and an augmentation of their sealift capability.

William P. Mako, Research Associate, wrote this book when he was a member of the Brookings Foreign Policy Studies program, which is directed by John D. Steinbruner. He is grateful to Robert Lucas Fischer, Phillip A. Karber, and Richard L. Kugler for helpful comments on the manuscript, to John J. Mearsheimer, Barry R. Posen, and James W. Shufelt for giving generously of their time to the project; and to his Brookings colleagues John C. Baker, Robert P. Berman, Richard K. Betts, and Bruce G. Blair for their encouragement and suggestions. Alice M. Carroll edited the manuscript, Alan G. Hoden verified its factual content, and Ann M. Ziegler and M. Cristina Gobin shared the secretarial support.

The Institution acknowledges the assistance of the Ford Foundation, whose grants helped support this study. The views expressed here are those of the author and should not be ascribed to the Ford Foundation, or to the trustees, officers, or other staff members of the Brookings Institution.

BRUCE K. MACLAURY
President

April 1983
Washington, D.C.

CONTENTS

1. **Introduction**   1
2. **Structure and Strength of U.S. Forces Since 1940**   3

    Mobilization for Global War, 1940–45   *3*
    Containment versus Mobilization, 1945–50   *6*
    Limited War I, 1950–53   *10*
    The New Look, 1953–60   *13*
    The Two-and-a Half-War Strategy, 1961–64   *16*
    Limited War II, 1965–68   *20*
    A One-and-a Half-War Strategy, 1969–78   *23*
    New Strains, Old Refrains   *27*

3. **Demands on Ground Forces in Central Europe in the 1980s**   31

    NATO's Central Front   *31*
    Ground Force Requirements   *35*
    Warsaw Pact Forces   *40*
    NATO Forces   *48*
    The Numerical Balance of Forces   *55*
    Other Factors   *58*

4. **Should the U.S. Contribution to NATO Change?**   65

    Increasing the U.S. Contribution   *65*
    Decreasing the U.S. Contribution   *73*
    Redirecting the U.S. Contribution   *79*
    Looking to the Allies   *85*
    Thinking about Military Specialization   *97*

5. **Conclusions**   101

Appendixes

A. Estimating Ground Combat Potential *105*
B. Composition of Warsaw Pact Fronts *126*
C. Composition of NATO Forces *131*

Index   135

Text Tables

2-1.	Strength of Active U.S. Ground Forces, Selected Years, 1940–80	4
2-2.	Location of Active U.S. Ground Force Divisions, Selected Years, 1945–80	8
2-3.	Strength of Reserve U.S. Ground Forces, Selected Years, 1950–80	9
2-4.	Mix Of Heavy and Light Divisions in the Active U.S. Force Structure, Selected years, 1945–80	17
3-1.	Warsaw Pact Deployments, 1980	42
3-2.	Readiness of Warsaw Pact Divisions in Selected Regions, by Category, 1980	44
3-3.	NATO's Ground Order of Battle for the Central Front	50
3-4.	Number of Men in Major Combat Units Available to NATO, at Selected Times after Mobilization Begins	54
4-1.	Reserve Establishments of Belgium, France, the Netherlands, and West Germany, 1980	89

Appendix Tables

A-1.	Personnel Strengths for Selected NATO Units	113
A-2.	Relative Value of Equipment in a U.S. Armored Division	114
A-3.	Relative Value of Equipment in a U.S. Mechanized Division	115
A-4.	Relative Value of Equipment in Units Attached to NATO Corps	116
A-5.	Relative Value of Equipment in a West German Armored Division	117
A-6.	Relative Value of Equipment in a West German Mechanized Division	118
A-7.	Relative Value of Equipment in a British Armored Division	119
A-8.	Relative Value of Equipment in a French Armored Division	120
A-9.	Relative Value of Equipment in a French Mechanized Division	120
A-10.	Relative Value of Equipment in a Soviet Armored Division	121
A-11.	Relative Value of Equipment in a Soviet Mechanized Division	122
A-12.	Relative Value of Equipment in an Eastern European Armored Division	123
A-13.	Relative Value of Equipment in an Eastern European Mechanized Division	124
A-14.	Relative Value of Equipment in Warsaw Pact Units held at Front or Army Level	125
C-1.	NATO Strength in Armored Division Equivalents, at Selected Times after Mobilization Begins	134

Figures

3-1. Corps Sectors of Military Responsibility on NATO's Central Front — 33
3-2. Pattern of Mobilization of NATO Forces and Proposed Alternatives — 57

CHAPTER ONE

INTRODUCTION

AMERICAN strategic thinking has long been built around the view that the security of Western Europe is vital to the security of the United States. This view reflects, among other things, an appreciation of Western Europe's economic resources, its liberal political values, and its cultural importance. Twice in this century, the United States has fought to preserve or free Western Europe from domination by a hostile power. And for several decades, it has accepted the risk of nuclear destruction and expended great resources to safeguard Western Europe's security against any threat from the Soviet Union. Currently, about 196,000 American troops are in West Germany to man or support a force equivalent to almost six divisions. The United States has further committed itself to a capability for sending six more divisions within two weeks of a decision to reinforce. The active and reserve forces contain another fourteen divisions and twenty-one brigades maintained principally to back up the forward-deployed forces and early reinforcements.

Should the United States retain this commitment—or increase it, reduce it, or somehow redirect it? Fresh consideration of this question, which is the focus of this study, is warranted by a combination of developments.[1] While remaining committed to aid in the defense of Western Europe and South Korea, in recent years the United States has assumed additional and perhaps more pressing responsibilities for defending key Western interests in Southwest Asia. Yet it has not significantly expanded its active or reserve ground forces to meet this further obligation. Moreover, the ability of the United States to make major

---

1. For previous examinations of the U.S. role, see John Newhouse and others, *U.S. Troops in Europe: Issues, Costs, and Choices* (Brookings Institution, 1971); Richard D. Lawrence and Jeffrey Record, *U.S. Force Structure in NATO: An Alternative* (Brookings Institution, 1974).

additions to its active ground forces—like those it made in the early 1960s—is now constrained by its ability to attract volunteers. Reinstitution of conscription, while favored by some observers, currently seems an unlikely possibility, barring a major crisis. At the same time that American power has been diluted, Soviet military power has grown steadily. Soviet gains in nuclear capability have raised further doubts about the credibility of the U.S. nuclear deterrent, while improvements in Soviet ground forces have, among other things, created concern about the amount of warning that would precede an invasion of Europe. Finally, political and economic factors—including the continued economic competitiveness of Western European countries and their uneven observance of 1977 pledges to raise defense spending—have helped rekindle American resentment over the share of the Western defense burden that the United States now bears. Proposals for a new division of labor are beginning to appear. Many envision an increased contribution of ground forces by allies of the United States; some contemplate a decreased or less demanding role for U.S. ground forces in plans for the defense of central Europe.

Subsequent chapters are meant to help the reader form reasoned opinions on the question of central concern here. Chapter 2 provides some historical perspective, in part through a review of the major decisions that shaped U.S. ground forces during the 1970s and which now leave some observers worried about their adequacy under a more demanding set of assumptions. It also recounts past instances of difficulty in balancing requirements for Europe against those for other contingencies and past problems in mobilizing the reserve components, a traditional response to demands for extra ground forces. Chapter 3 examines the military equation as it applies to conventional warfare in central Europe. Chapter 4 presents, along with opposing views, specific proposals for changing the Western side of the central European equation.

CHAPTER TWO

STRUCTURE AND STRENGTH OF U.S. FORCES SINCE 1940

THE DRIVING FORCE in the development of U.S. ground forces over the past four decades has normally been preparation for general war in Europe. Repeatedly, tensions have arisen between these preparations for general war and the requirements for deterring or prosecuting limited wars. Concern about the threat of general war in Europe has sometimes worked to degrade the United States' capabilities for waging a limited war, while the prosecution of limited wars has periodically caused significant distortions of the overall posture of U.S. ground forces. Because the designated levels of manpower and equipment for U.S. reserve forces have seldom been met, it has not been possible to resolve these conflicts by rapid mobilization of reserves. These are tendencies that have endured through forty years of changing U.S. defense policy, and they are likely to continue to have a strong influence on ground force posture.

Mobilization for Global War, 1940–45

Between 1940 and 1945, the U.S. Army and Marine Corps underwent the greatest expansion in their history. By 1945, personnel strength was twenty-two times what it had been in 1940 (see table 2-1). The mobilization that produced this vast increase did not reach a crescendo until 1942. Despite a deteriorating situation in both Europe and Asia, mobilization proceeded by fits and starts until December 1941, principally because the Roosevelt administration feared posing an overt challenge to isolationist sentiment in this country.[1]

1. Russell F. Weigley, *History of the United States Army* (Macmillan, 1967), pp. 430–32.

4   Defense of Central Europe

Table 2-1. Strength of Active U.S. Ground Forces, Selected Years, 1940–80

Year	Army		Marine Corps		Total	
	Thousands of men	Divisions[a]	Thousands of men	Divisions	Thousands of men	Divisions
1940	264[b]	8	28	0[c]	292	8
1945	5,912[b]	89	485	6	6,397	95
1950	591	10	75	2	666	12
1953	1,534	20	249	3	1,783	23
1960	873	14	171	3	1,044	17
1962	1,066	18	191	3	1,257	21
1964	972	16	190	3	1,162	19
1968	1,570	19[d]	307	4	1,877	23
1972	811	13	198	3	1,009	16
1976	779	16	192	3	971	19
1980	774	16	189	3	963	19

Sources: *Selected Manpower Statistics,* selected years; *Department of Defense Annual Report,* selected years; U.S. Army Command and General Staff College, *Selected Readings in the Evolution of Combat Formations* (Fort Leavenworth, Kan.: USACGSC, 1968), vol. 2, pp. 3/25, 7/1; Russell F. Weigley, *History of the United States Army* (Macmillan, 1967), pp. 438, 502; William D. Parker, *A Concise History of the United States Marine Corps, 1775–1969* (U.S. Government Printing Office, 1970), pp. 74, 77, 139.

a. In addition, the Army has always maintained a varying number of separate brigades and regiments.
b. Excludes Army Air Corps.
c. Until World War II, brigades were the largest formation in the Marine Corps.
d. Includes Americal division, a composite of combat and support units.

Not surprisingly, mobilization on so grand a scale encountered numerous difficulties. Among other things, the reserve components took a long time to achieve combat readiness.[2] This was partly due to the state of the reserves at the start of mobilization. In addition to being poorly equipped, on average the eighteen infantry divisions of the National Guard were 50 percent understrength when called into federal service. The twenty-six divisions of the Army Reserve were simply paper units, usually without equipment or personnel. Reserve divisions from both components had to be filled out with raw recruits, and most divisions repeatedly lost trained personnel to meet the continuous demand for combat replacements, officer candidates, training cadres, and so forth. Constant personnel turnover caused monthly fluctuations in the combat readiness of reserve divisions forming for battle. Those few National Guard divisions that were kept relatively intact from

2. But far more important than the time needed to achieve combat readiness in the deployment of U.S. ground forces overseas were the availability of shipping, equipment shortages, and strategic indecision. Data used here on reserve mobilization are from U.S. Army Command and General Staff College, *Selected Readings in the Evolution of Combat Formations* (Fort Leavenworth, Kan.: USACGSC, 1968), vol. 2, pp. 3/11–3/14.

activation to deployment took on average eleven months to become combat-ready, and the Army Reserve divisions likewise took thirteen months. (Notably, one Army division that was raised from scratch was able to deploy just twelve months after activation.)

The U.S. effort to mobilize combat divisions suffered from continual shortages of manpower, trained or otherwise. In the fall of 1941, it was assumed that defeat of the Axis powers would require a U.S. ground force of about 9 million men, organized into more than 200 divisions. The combined strength of the Army (including the Army Air Force) and Marine Corps did in fact reach 8,765,000 by mid-1945. But the United States never managed to raise anything on the order of 200 divisions.[3] Global lines of communication and American standards for mechanization and completeness of supply required the service of unanticipated numbers of soldiers in support units. Geography and the need to fight in some manner while ground divisions were still forming produced a heavy emphasis on air and sea power, which further limited the Army's manpower pool,[4] as did the requirements of a large industrial base, needed to meet the materiel demands of the United States and its allies. In the end, the United States created fewer divisions than did most of the other major belligerents,[5] ending up with 95, almost three-quarters of which were deployed in Europe. By early 1945, no strategic reserve remained in the United States. The last American divisions had already been dispatched, and no more were forming. Overseas, no significant reserves of U.S. ground forces were to be found in any of the theaters of operation. From a strategic standpoint, one Army historian suggests, the United States experienced "a fairly narrow escape from disagreeable eventualities, in case general strategic plans had suffered a serious setback."[6]

But as a cushion against its mobilization problems, the United States had the strength of its allies. In particular, an adequately equipped Soviet

3. For a discussion of the Army's manpower requirements and problems, see Maurice Matloff, "The 90-Division Gamble," in Kent Roberts Greenfield, ed., *Command Decisions*, a vol. of *The United States Army in World War II* (U.S. Government Printing Office, 1960), pp. 365–81.

4. Weigley, *History of the United States Army*, p. 437.

5. The Soviet Union raised some 400 divisions, Germany about 300, and Japan about 100.

6. Robert R. Palmer, "Mobilization of the Ground Army," in Kent Roberts Greenfield, Robert R. Palmer, and Bell I. Wiley, *The Organization of Ground Combat Troops*, vol. 1 of *The United States Army in World War II* (Historical Division, Department of the Army, 1947), pp. 193, 195.

Army tied down numerous Axis formations in Europe and the Far East. And U.S. naval strength "made it possible for American ground forces to attack at advantageous times and places," while air power "enabled ground forces to attack an enemy underequipped, disrupted, and sometimes immobilized."[7] In addition, American ground forces possessed weapons, equipment, and transport in such quantities that they could overwhelm enemies with sheer weight of firepower and count on adequate logistical support in every theater of operations.[8] Although shipping shortages did slow the movement of U.S. ground forces overseas, American superiority in strategic mobility was still so great that U.S. divisions "could be shifted wherever they were needed with a promptness that no other army could match."[9] Finally, geographical distance effectively eliminated the threat of attack on the American homeland.

Containment versus Mobilization, 1945–50

America's demobilization at the end of World War II could well be characterized as an organized rout. By 1948, the combined personnel strength of the Army and Marine Corps was less than one-tenth of the peak level reached in 1945. The pace of demobilization was forced on a reluctant Truman administration by a feeling—predominant among Congress, the public, and the troops themselves—that, the pendulum having swung from total war to total peace, there was no justification for keeping men in the armed forces against their will. American diplomats complained that precipitate demobilization made it difficult for them to be firm with Moscow in negotiations on a postwar order during the first eighteen months after the war. For this reason, some observers later lamented the rapidity of the U.S. demobilization. Yet, as Harvard professor Samuel Huntington argues, the citizen army raised for total war would have been ill suited to the demands of cold war, and the decks had to be quickly cleared to make way for something more appropriate.[10]

7. Ibid., p. 190.

8. Today the United States emphasizes quality of war materiel, but during World War II it managed to put its productive capacity to good use by "a deliberate decision, to sacrifice sometimes the possibility of creating the very best materiel in order to get weapons and equipment into prompt mass production." Weigley, *History of the United States Army*, p. 479.

9. Ibid.

10. Samuel P. Huntington, *The Common Defense: Strategic Programs in National Politics* (Columbia University Press, 1961), pp. 36–38.

When the United States embraced the containment of communism as a foreign policy, in early 1948, the resulting expansion of its peacetime security perimeter—from the eastern Pacific and western Atlantic to an area including substantial territories around the Eurasian periphery—presented the United States with a host of new threats. In central Europe, 12 scattered and understrength Western divisions were assumed to be facing a Soviet force of 25 divisions backed by another 115–150 divisions in the Soviet Union, all at full battle strength. Despite the militancy of Stalin's foreign policy, however, "there was no significant fear of a massive Soviet invasion"; the greater concern was that the nations of Western Europe, prostrate and demoralized from the war, would fall prey to communist subversion and infiltration.[11] As for elsewhere along the line, a number of American officials pointed to the threat of communist probes and "brushfire wars" in such places as Greece, Turkey, Palestine, Iran, and Korea.

Ground forces were required to back up a policy of containment. By 1950, however, active U.S. ground forces consisted of just twelve divisions, all but one of them badly understrength, ill equipped, and lacking in logistical support. The United States maintained only one division in Europe (table 2-2) which, along with an American constabulary force, participated in the occupation of Germany. In the Far East it had just four Army divisions (at 65 percent strength) occupying Japan, all U.S. ground units having returned from China and Korea in 1949. With a strategic reserve amounting to only seventy thousand soldiers and marines, one Army general warned that the employment overseas of any force larger than a division would have required partial mobilization.[12]

This disjunction between foreign policy and ground force posture, according to Huntington, was due to both domestic political circumstances and narrow military thinking.[13] Although draft authority was restored in June 1948, after having lapsed in March 1947, budgetary limits severely constrained U.S. ground force programs until 1950. Over Truman's objections, a Republican Congress pushed a major tax cut through in 1948. Domestic expenditures, foreign aid programs, and interest payments—coupled with Truman's determination to maintain a balanced budget—left little money for military programs. While admit-

---

11. Robert Endicott Osgood, *NATO: The Entangling Alliance* (University of Chicago Press, 1962), pp. 28–30.
12. Huntington, *Common Defense*, p. 40.
13. Ibid., pp. 41–43.

Table 2-2. Location of Active U.S. Ground Force Divisions, Selected Years, 1945–80

Year	Number in		
	Continental United States	Europe	Asia and Pacific
1945	0	69	26
1950	7	1	4
1953	9	5	9
1960	8	5	4
1962	12	5	4
1964	10	5	4
1968	6	5[a]	12[b]
1972	9	4	3
1976	12	4	3
1980	12	4	3

Sources: USACGSC, *Selected Readings*, vol. 1, pp. 2/58–2/59, and vol. 2, p. 3/40; Weigley, *History of the United States Army*, pp. 502, 508; Parker, *A Concise History*, pp. 74, 77; *Department of Defense Annual Report*, selected years; International Institute for Strategic Studies, *The Military Balance* (London: IISS), selected years.
a. One of these returned to the United States during 1968.
b. Includes Americal division, a composite of combat and support units.

ting the desirability of a stronger military posture, especially after the Soviet atomic test and Chinese Communist victory in 1949, the Truman administration again felt compelled to go along with public and congressional desires for an austere defense program.

But ground forces more appropriate for deterring communist expansionism could have been created, the State Department's George Kennan argued, had U.S. military doctrine not been so preoccupied with preparing for a general war in Europe.[14] At that time, Americans tended to identify war with total war. Because budgetary constraints precluded the maintenance of a large standing army oriented toward Western Europe's defense, the main emphasis in ground force planning was on building a capability for full-scale mobilization like that in World War II. As the postwar shape of the reserves was being debated, with proposals for universal military training producing much controversy, a force structure for the Army's reserve components emerged that bore a curious resemblance to that of the 1930s (table 2-3). The Army Reserve's prewar structure of twenty-six divisions was restored, and again the Reserve became largely a paper organization. The National Guard was expanded to twenty-seven divisions, with a higher proportion of support units than in the 1930s, but not enough to complement all the divisions. By 1950, the National Guard had only about half its required equipment and was

14. Ibid., pp. 43–44.

Table 2-3. **Strength of Reserve U.S. Ground Forces, Selected Years, 1950–80**

Year	Army National Guard		Army Reserve		Marine Corps Reserve		Total	
	Thousands of men	Divisions	Thousands of men	Divisions	Thousands of men	Divisions	Thousands of men	Divisions
1950	325	27	187	26	40	0	552	53
1953	256	19[a]	117	26	20	0	393	45
1960	402	27	301	10	45	0	748	37
1962	361	25[b]	310	10	49	0	720	35
1964	382	23	269	6	46	1	697	30
1968	389	8	244	0	47	1	680	9
1972	388	8	235	0	41	1	664	9
1976	362	8	195	0	30	1	587	9
1980	365	8	200	0	34	1	599	9

Sources: USACGSC, *Selected Readings*, vol. 2, p. 3/25. *Semiannual Report of the Secretary of Defense, January 1 to June 30, 1950*, p. 208; *July 1 to December 31, 1953*, p. 53. *Annual Report of the Secretary of Defense, July 1, 1959 to June 30, 1960*, p. 416. *Department of Defense Annual Report for Fiscal Year 1962*, p. 391; *Fiscal Year 1963*, p. 28; *Fiscal Year 1968*, p. 40; *Fiscal Year 1980*, p. B/4.
a. Excludes 8 divisions federalized for the Korean War.
b. Excludes 2 divisions federalized for the Berlin crisis.

some forty thousand men below its authorized strength—an authorized strength that was, in any case, insufficient to fill all the units. The reserve structure thus included fifty-three divisions, but these forces were not expected to be able to reach their military potential until one or two years after the start of a general mobilization. Significantly, there was little or no planning for partial mobilization.[15]

While planning for full-scale mobilization, the United States increased its commitment to the defense of Western Europe by acceding to the North Atlantic Treaty in 1949. Some domestic supporters of the treaty argued it would greatly decrease the chances of any challenge to the balance of power in Europe. The United States moved also to strengthen its strategic nuclear forces, providing a nuclear umbrella over Europe that many Americans saw as a deterrent to Soviet aggression.[16] This emphasis on strategic nuclear capabilities reflected the relative ease with which the United States could project air power and accorded with the first unified defense plan of the North Atlantic Treaty Organization. The NATO plan, agreed to in January 1950, embodied the concept of "collective balanced forces," with each country specializing in the kinds of military forces for which it was best suited, within an integrated defense structure. The United States was to concentrate on strategic air

15. USACGSC, *Selected Readings*, pp. 3/14–3/15.
16. Huntington, *Common Defense*, pp. 313–14.

power and naval forces, "while Europe was to provide the 'hard core of ground power in being.'"[17]

The Truman administration recognized that the American ground posture it had accepted entailed substantial military risks in the short term. Although the North Atlantic Treaty (along with the Marshall Plan) demonstrably reduced Western Europe's vulnerability to political warfare, it did nothing to redress a perceived military imbalance. It was simply assumed that nothing could prevent a massive Soviet assault from overrunning Western Europe at least to the Pyrenees.[18] Elsewhere too the U.S. ground posture was not strong enough to deter communist aggression. The Truman administration worried about these risks but hesitated to undertake a campaign to reshape public opinion on national security. While the first comprehensive statement of national strategy, NSC-68 issued in 1950, urged an expansion of U.S. and allied capabilities for both general and limited war, it did not anticipate communist aggression before 1954, when the Soviet Union was expected to have nuclear forces in operation.[19]

Limited War I, 1950–53

The communist attack on South Korea in June 1950 abruptly changed the Truman administration's priorities and timetables. The United States suddenly decided that South Korea could not be abandoned to piecemeal aggression and discovered that the South Korean army was utterly incapable of defending the country. It soon dispatched three under-strength, ill-equipped, and poorly trained divisions from the occupation force in Japan. Prompt and heavy U.S. air support is credited with having enabled these and allied formations to hang onto the southern tip of Korea until enough reinforcements arrived to solidify the Pusan perimeter and then permit a counteroffensive.[20] The initial reinforce-

17. Osgood, *NATO*, pp. 45–47.
18. Ibid., p. 29.
19. Executive Secretary on United States Objectives and Programs for National Security, "NSC-68: A Report to the National Security Council" (April 14, 1950); reprinted in *Naval War College Review* (May–June 1975), pp. 61, 66–67, 82.
20. According to General Walton Walker, commander of the U.S. Army in Korea, "if it had not been for the air support that we received from the [U.S. Air Force] we would not have been able to stay in Korea." Robert Frank Futrell, *The United States Air Force in Korea, 1950–53* (Duell, Sloan and Pearce, 1961), pp. 138–39. For operational details, see ibid., pp. 85–87, 90–92, 132–38.

ments from the United States, individuals and units who rounded out or augmented the weak American divisions in Korea, left the U.S. strategic reserve badly depleted and disorganized for a while. By 1953, U.S. combat forces in Korea comprised eight Army divisions and one Marine division.

While requirements for the war in Korea received the greatest immediate emphasis, the United States also set out to improve its ground posture vis-à-vis Western Europe. An increase in the U.S. ground presence there had been considered before; NSC-68 had questioned the value of U.S. nuclear forces as a deterrent to invasion after the Soviet Union eventually acquired similar capabilities. During the fall of 1950, a communist attack on Europe suddenly seemed imminent. For apart from demonstrating a willingness to use force in the pursuit of its goals, the assault on South Korea appeared to invalidate the assumption that the Soviet bloc would not commit outright aggression until the Soviet Union had acquired a significant nuclear capability. The goal of collective balanced forces for NATO was dropped in favor of integrated forces under U.S. command, and in 1951 four U.S. divisions were deployed to West Germany, partly to induce European rearmament. This reintroduction of a major U.S. ground presence into Europe may have been the most important, long-lasting effect of the Korean conflict. While reinforcing its ground deployments on the Continent, the United States engaged in a general buildup of its ground forces, the effect of which was to increase the number of active ground formations potentially available for a general war in Europe. By 1953, it had fourteen active divisions in Europe or in its strategic reserve, in contrast to eight in 1950.

To build up these forces, the United States began a limited mobilization of its reserve components in July 1950. The administration, suspicious that the attack on Korea was a diversionary prelude to a worldwide offensive, decided to concentrate initially on calling up individual reservists—mostly World War II veterans—from the volunteer and inactive lists, while leaving the organized reserve units to provide a hedge against contingencies elsewhere. Some members of reserve units were called, however, to serve as fillers or as combat replacements, and in September 1950 some National Guard units were mobilized. By March 1952, it had become necessary to mobilize eight National Guard divisions, of which two went to Korea and two to Germany.

Because previous planning had focused so on total mobilization, limited mobilization meant that both reservists and reserve units had to be called on an impromptu basis, as needs arose. As members of organized units were drafted to provide fillers and replacements, the integrity and readiness of these reserve units were degraded. Federalized National Guard units took fifteen to seventeen months to achieve combat readiness before they could be deployed, in part because their peacetime strengths were so low—on average, the four National Guard divisions eventually sent overseas had only 46 percent of their authorized personnel when called to service. Another factor was personnel turnover, an experience the reserves shared with all U.S.-based Army divisions (except an airborne division), which were used for training and as sources of replacements. Hence, it was very difficult to determine the length of time a unit needed to achieve true readiness. Finally, among the reservists called from the volunteer and inactive lists were many war veterans, who were hardly aware of any reserve obligation and regarded their recall to service as "double jeopardy." The problems of both individuals and units were largely due to the absence of any sizable pool of individual reinforcements within the active or reserve forces in 1950.[21]

As it ran into some problems, limited mobilization created others. Because Korea was not an all-out war, there was no need to mobilize all the nation's manpower. Consequently, the dangers and burdens of wartime service could hardly be distributed in a fair manner. The World War II veterans were especially apt to question why they should serve, but the inequities seemed just as great to members of federalized reserve units, which were drawn from particular locales (the two National Guard divisions sent to Korea came from California and Oklahoma). Attempts to minimize the unfairness of limited mobilization are said to have complicated prosecution of the war. A rotation system that the Army adopted produced such rapid turnover of personnel that formations fighting in Korea never achieved much cohesion.[22] Dissatisfaction with the inequities of mobilization compounded growing public disillusionment with the kind of war being waged in Korea, limited war being a concept still alien to most Americans.[23] These feelings contributed to the political undoing of the Truman administration.

21. USACGSC, *Selected Readings,* pp. 3/15–3/18, 3/41.
22. Weigley, *History of the United States Army,* pp. 508–11.
23. Even the Army viewed Korea as a "unique" experience that should not distract the Army from its primary concern with preparations for general war in Europe. Huntington, *Common Defense,* p. 344.

Between 1950 and 1953, U.S. ground forces nearly tripled in size. While operations in Korea consumed much of this growth and caused readiness problems for the strategic reserve, the United States managed to quintuple its ground combat force in Europe. This increase did encourage some expansion of allied armies. But Western ground forces in Europe in no way approached the seventy-five-division goal set by NATO at its 1952 Lisbon conference. As fear of imminent Soviet aggression subsided, so did any inclination to meet the Lisbon goals, thus leaving assessments of the European balance almost as gloomy as before. In retrospect, Osgood suggests, "it seems unwarranted to have inferred an imminent danger of Soviet aggression in Europe from the North Korean attack upon a peripheral strategic position in the Far East, especially since the United States had withdrawn her troops from Korea and publicly excluded it from her 'defensive perimeter.'"[24] One might add that South Korea's exclusion was intended to free scarce assets for concentration on Europe's behalf, and ask why America's manifest determination to wage an unpopular effort to resecure what had just been dismissed as strategically irrelevant never figured in NATO's deterrence calculations. However, "the estimate of a potential aggressor's intentions is peculiarly subject to sudden shifts from complacency to alarm."[25] Whatever the merits of the decision to return to Europe in force, American deployments there were to remain fairly constant over the next decade.

The New Look, 1953–60

Soon after taking office, the Eisenhower administration introduced a "new look" in U.S. defense policy. Convinced that national security programs had to be balanced against the requirements for a strong economy, the administration set out to cut taxes, balance the budget, and reduce military expenditures to a level sustainable over "the long haul." Far from making any retreat from its position in the world, the United States actually expanded its formal alliance commitments during the early years of the Eisenhower administration. Increased American reliance on nuclear weapons was the key feature of the New Look. In

24. *NATO*, pp. 68–69, 87.
25. Ibid., p. 69.

late 1953, dismissing the possibility that another sizable conflict would be fought with conventional weapons alone, the Eisenhower administration authorized the services to plan on using nuclear weapons whenever deemed militarily desirable. Its main intention was to forestall Army formulation of large manpower and materiel requirements based on preparations for a repeat of World War II or Korea. This decision set the stage for unprecedented public emphasis on America's readiness to retaliate—massively or otherwise—with nuclear weapons against any communist aggression. And the threat amounted to more than just a bluff. By 1954, the U.S. deployment of tactical nuclear weapons had begun, and plans for Western Europe's defense had been altered to give strategic air power the decisive role. The greater emphasis on strategic air power reflected official support for "collective balanced forces." Although it never intended to respond with nuclear weapons to every minor encounter, the administration—not wanting to see America progressively weakened by a series of Koreas—was determined to use nuclear weapons "in a wider range of contingencies than those for which the previous administration had firmly planned."[26]

One standard review of this period suggests that the New Look had more of an impact on operational doctrine than on military programs.[27] Although the United States refrained from rapid demobilization after the 1953 Korean cease-fire, its ground forces did undergo successive reductions. By 1960, their active personnel strength had been cut more than one-third below the peak level reached during the Korean War; and the number of Army divisions had been reduced from twenty to fourteen (three of which were actually training divisions). These reductions, however, were not as radical as the logic of national strategy might have dictated. The 1956 Radford plan to cut the Army to 550,000 men, a number lower than the 1950 level, and reduce the U.S. ground presence overseas to just a token force in Europe was never adopted. So as not to upset its allies, the United States also continued to maintain five divisions in Europe and at least four in Asia and the Pacific, including two in South Korea, whose own army was now much stronger than it had been in 1950. Finally, having officially accepted by 1955 the need for "versatile, ready forces to cope with limited aggression" so as never to have "to

26. Glenn H. Snyder, "The 'New Look' of 1953," in Warner R. Schilling, Paul Y. Hammond, and Glenn H. Snyder, *Strategy, Politics, and Defense Budgets* (Columbia University Press, 1962), pp. 436–37, 467–68, 484–85, 492–93.
27. Ibid., pp. 492–93.

choose between yielding to local aggression or applying the undiscriminating power of nuclear destruction,"[28] the administration allowed the military services to take many specific steps—within imposed budgetary restrictions—to meet the threat of limited war. For instance, in 1958 the Army created the Strategic Army Corps and assigned four U.S.-based divisions to it. Personnel reductions did force the Army to cut these to three divisions in 1959. The Marines, however, continued to contribute three divisions to American capabilities for limited war, even though the corps' personnel strength declined somewhat after Korea. The Marines' performance in Korea and growing irritation at continual attempts by the executive to cut the corps had led Congress to pass legislation in 1952 requiring a minimum Marine force structure of three divisions.

While making its cutbacks, the Eisenhower administration maintained, at least in public, that improvements in reserve readiness could adequately compensate for decreases in active troop levels. The administration originated the Reserve Forces Act of 1955 which, by initiating three to six months of active-duty training for men entering the reserves without prior service, freed reserve units from having to devote most of their training time to basic training. The administration also pushed through a reorganization intended to increase reserve readiness by concentrating more reservists in a smaller number of units. The fate of this reorganization, however, indicates both the administration's foremost interest in finding a cheap replacement for those active forces being cut and the political strength of the reserve establishment. Since low peacetime manning levels had slowed attainment of combat readiness by the reserve units mobilized for World War II and Korea, in 1954 the Defense Department proposed raising the total paid-drill strength of the National Guard and Army Reserve to 1,267,000 men and cutting their force structure to 37 divisions (the Guard would retain 27 while the Reserve would go from 26 to 10 divisions), a size judged suitable for this paid-drill strength. Planning continued through 1955 on the basis of this proposal. In 1956 the secretary of defense arbitrarily set a total paid-drill strength of 630,000 as a goal for the reserves. Congress objected, however, and arbitrarily set the figure at 700,000. Because this level was considered too low to support a 37-division structure, the Army in 1957 proposed a 27-division structure. Leaders of the reserves, Congress, and state governments all objected, however, and the 37-division struc-

28. Maxwell D. Taylor, *The Uncertain Trumpet* (Harper, 1960), pp. 26–27.

ture was retained despite the shortfall in resources committed. The Defense Department subsequently adopted a system of priorities to balance early and later mobilization needs, but even high-priority reserve units reportedly remained substantially understrength in men and equipment and incapable of meeting their mobilization goals.[29]

Although the United States retained more ground capability than was perhaps consistent with national strategy and, indeed, faced no further military challenges to its interests after the Korean cease-fire, by 1960 the emphasis on a nuclear strategy was wearing thin. Dramatic advances in the Soviet Union's nuclear capabilities were prompting serious doubts about the deterrent value of U.S. nuclear forces. Was the United States willing to risk its own nuclear destruction to hold the line in Asia or even in Europe? While critics focused on this credibility question, the defenders of national strategy continued to argue that the capability alone for massive nuclear retaliation provided an overwhelming deterrent to aggression. The American emphasis on nuclear weapons, however, did discourage the Western Europeans from building up their conventional forces, according to Osgood. Hence, against an unchanged view of the Soviet threat, the conventional balance in Europe continued to look abysmal.[30]

The Two-and-a-Half-War Strategy, 1961–64

The Kennedy administration entered office believing that the U.S. emphasis on nuclear weapons could no longer offset military threats from the Soviet Union and China, given Moscow's advances in nuclear arms. Soviet promises of support for "wars of national liberation" also soon caused U.S. officials to worry much more about the threat of limited war. All this led the new administration to adopt a "two-and-a-half-war" strategy that postulated a requirement for enough forces to wage, simultaneously, a three-month conventional forward defense of Western Europe, a defense of South Korea or Southeast Asia against a

---

29. USACGSC, *Selected Readings*, pp. 3/18–3/20.
30. By 1958, Western forces in central Europe amounted to fewer than 20 effective divisions. Official NATO estimates showed 175 Soviet divisions, of which 140 were combat-ready (including 22 in East Germany and Poland and about 80 in western Russia and the rest of Eastern Europe), and a capability for mobilizing 400 divisions in thirty days. Osgood, *NATO,* pp. 104, 118.

Table 2-4. Mix of Heavy and Light Divisions in the Active U.S. Force Structure, Selected Years, 1945–80

Unit	1945	1950	1953	1960	1962	1964	1968	1972	1976	1980
Heavy divisions	16	1	2	3	9	8	8	7	9	10
Armored	16	1	2	3	5	4	4	3	4	4
Mechanized infantry	0	0	0	0	4	4	4	4	5	6
Light divisions	79	11	21	14	12	11	15	9	10	9
Infantry	68[a]	7	16	9	7	6	8	3	5	4
Airborne	5	2	2	2	2	2	1	2[b]	1	1
Air mobile	0	0	0	0	0	0	2	1[c]	1	1
Marine	6	2	3	3	3	3	4	3	3	3
Total divisions	95	12	23	17	21	19	23	16	19	19
Heavy divisions as a percent of total	17	8	9	18	43	42	35	44	47	53

Sources: USACGSC, *Selected Readings*, vol. 2, pp. 3/11–3/16; *Department of Defense Annual Report*, selected years; IISS, *Military Balance*, selected years.
a. Includes 1 mountain and 1 cavalry division.
b. Includes 1 air-portable division.
c. Experimental division, with 1 armored brigade, 1 air-mobile infantry brigade, and 1 air cavalry combat brigade.

full-scale Chinese attack, and a minor operation somewhere else.[31] This strategy generated plans for increasing the strategic reserve of active ground forces and for improving the readiness of the reserve components.

The Berlin crisis of 1961, however, prompted a number of immediate moves to strengthen the U.S. ground posture vis-à-vis Europe. The three training divisions in the active Army were brought up to full strength and made combat-ready. About 42,000 troops were sent to Europe, mostly to provide the U.S. Army in Europe with the combat and support units necessary for sustained conventional operations that had been lacking since the Army's 1956 reorganization for nuclear combat. The three infantry divisions in West Germany were mechanized and additional heavy divisions in the United States were activated, so that the ratio of heavy to light divisions in the ground forces was substantially increased. This significant departure from past preferences in the mix of active divisions (table 2-4) was prompted by a belief that heavy formations were most appropriate for Europe (given the greater protection that armored vehicles afforded in a nuclear war and the mechanization that Soviet ground forces underwent in the late 1950s).[32]

31. Alain C. Enthoven and K. Wayne Smith, *How Much Is Enough? Shaping the Defense Program, 1961–1969* (Harper and Row, 1971), pp. 214–15.
32. The Army considered creating fully motorized infantry divisions in World War II. But their bulk and shortages of shipping led the Army to drop these formations in favor of the somewhat less mobile, traditional infantry divisions.

To facilitate the deployment of U.S.-based heavy formations, the equipment for two divisions was also prepositioned in Europe. At the height of the crisis, a limited mobilization was carried out in which 119,000 Army reservists were called up, including those from the two National Guard divisions (from Wisconsin and Texas) that were federalized.

Again the call-up of reservists and reserve units created problems. Despite the Korean experience, military plans were still shaped in terms of general mobilization, which again produced many uncertainties and last-minute changes of direction. The two National Guard divisions called to service had only about 70 percent of their authorized manpower when federalized and hence took at least six months to achieve combat readiness. Rather than take people from unmobilized reserve units, an expedient that had degraded the readiness of such units during the Korean mobilization, the Army relied on the pool of individual ready reservists inherited from the Eisenhower administration for individual fillers. But many of them were unaware of any reserve obligation or could not be located.[33] And the limited scope of this mobilization again caused resentment among those called to duty and raised "questions about the fairness of the selection for service, with Congress among the questioners."[34] Apart from confirming the administration's belief that a larger strategic reserve of active ground forces was necessary, the Berlin mobilization suggested a need for plans for a limited mobilization, including a clear designation of the units to be called first in various contingencies.

Although the Soviet campaign of political warfare in Europe was unsettling, the Kennedy administration believed that military challenges to American security were more likely to arise in the form of local conflicts. Hence, it also took steps to improve U.S. capabilities for waging a limited war. The active personnel strength of the Marine Corps was raised and the size of the Special Forces, the Army's counterinsurgency specialists, was increased eightfold. An expanded Strategic Army Corps was left with eight divisions organized into two corps—one essentially airborne, the other strong in armor. With a 75 percent increase in its airlift capabilities, it could "quickly provide a reinforced infantry company or a complete corps to handle a crisis in any part of the globe," giving the United States "great flexibility to deal with multiple situations

33. USACGSC, *Selected Readings,* pp. 3/20–3/23, 3/44.
34. Ibid., p. 3/22; Weigley, *History of the United States Army,* p. 531.

in widely separated areas."[35] In 1961, the administration also established Strike Command, a joint body designed to coordinate the Army's and Air Force's planning for limited war, which had been lacking since the creation of the Strategic Army Corps in 1958. The Middle East served as a particular focus for Strike Command's planning and exercises. In the Far East, the United States tried prepositioning ground equipment aboard ships. Finally, in part to back up its limited war capabilities, the administration set out to improve reserve readiness.

Soon after entering office, the Kennedy administration had concluded that the mission of the reserve forces was obscure and that their size and structure were the product of pure happenstance rather than sound planning. The new administration wanted from the reserve components an ability to replenish the strategic reserve promptly if active forces were committed to a local conflict, so that the United States could remain ready to meet other commitments.[36] And with a 45 percent increase in the number of combat divisions and a mere 10 percent growth in personnel strength between 1960 and 1964, the active Army was dependent on its reserve components for logistical and training support in any emergency. The administration's 1963 reserve reorganization plan called for eliminating four National Guard divisions, four Army Reserve divisions, and many smaller units so that resources could be concentrated on fewer units in hopes of raising their readiness. In order to concentrate resources still further, this reorganization also divided the Army's reserve components into an Immediate Reserve—of eight Guard divisions, eleven brigades, and support elements, all manned at 70–80 percent strength and assigned readiness objectives ranging from a few hours to twelve weeks—and a Reinforcing Reserve consisting of all other units, with lower manning levels and longer readiness objectives.[37] Although the Congress and state governments opposed the elimination of reserve units, the administration managed to carry out this realignment largely as planned, presumably because a cogent rationale was behind its

---

35. *Department of Defense Annual Report for Fiscal Year 1964*, p. 3; *Fiscal Year 1963*, p. 109.

36. William W. Kaufmann, *The McNamara Strategy* (Harper and Row, 1964), pp. 63–64. The creation of a Marine Corps Reserve division was an obvious product of this concept. Previously, the Marine Corps Reserve had been a loose organization, oriented toward providing individual replacements for active units in wartime.

37. *Department of Defense Annual Report for Fiscal Year 1963*, p. 123; *Fiscal Year 1964*, p. 3.

proposal and because memories of the difficult Berlin mobilization were still fresh.

Despite all these improvements, by 1964 the United States had not acquired the forces believed needed for fighting major wars in Europe and Asia while simultaneously waging a minor operation somewhere else.[38] The prospects for a conventional forward defense of Western Europe had brightened considerably, however. While the United States' ground forces were undergoing improvement, West Germany continued to progress toward completion of its rearmament program; the objective threat from the Soviet Army remained at a lower level after the cuts Khrushchev made between 1955 and 1960; and assessments of the threat posed by the Warsaw Pact armies revealed that their divisions were smaller and weaker than their American counterparts, lacked staying power, and were normally manned at reduced or merely cadre strength.[39] As for limited war, increases in the strategic reserve of combat-ready divisions as well as other programs had given the United States a greater capability for dealing with local conflicts. Finally, improvements in the reserves had left them more ready to respond to major or minor contingencies.

Limited War II, 1965–68

In 1965, the first U.S. ground combat units were deployed to South Vietnam and the American buildup for war in Southeast Asia began. By 1968, the active personnel strength of U.S. ground forces was more than 60 percent higher than it had been in 1964 and had surpassed the level of 1953. Indeed, by 1968, ten U.S. divisions as well as several independent brigades and regiments were engaged in Vietnam, a larger force than had fought in Korea. The way in which these forces were gathered, however, is widely judged to have had a profoundly deleterious impact on the overall U.S. ground posture.

Despite the efforts of the Kennedy and Johnson administrations to improve the readiness of the reserve components to replenish the

38. Richard M. Nixon, *U.S. Foreign Policy for the 1970s: A New Strategy for Peace*, a report to the Congress (U.S. Government Printing Office, 1970), pp. 128–29. See also Maxwell D. Taylor, "Changing Military Priorities," *AEI Foreign Policy and Defense Review*, vol. 1 (April 1979), p. 8.

39. For the classic account of this reassessment, see Enthoven and Smith, *How Much Is Enough?* pp. 132–42.

strategic reserve and to support the active forces in any conflict, the reserves were not called when an appropriate hour struck. In July 1965, the Johnson administration decided that Vietnam requirements would be met through the creation of new active formations and the absorption of draftees, while units in the reserve components were saved for other contingencies or for future needs in Southeast Asia. By 1966, high-priority reserve units had reportedly attained unprecedented levels of premobilization readiness.[40] Why were they not immediately called? The usual explanation is that the Johnson administration—presumably mindful of the resentment that the limited mobilizations for Korea and Berlin had stirred—did not want to heighten popular discontent with another limited war.[41] A largely symbolic mobilization, involving the call-up of 18,500 soldiers from the Guard and Reserve, eventually was carried out, during the spring of 1968, in response to the *Pueblo* crisis and Tet offensive.

In addition to causing the U.S. strategic reserve to shrink from ten to five or six divisions by 1968,[42] the administration's refusal to order a limited mobilization in 1965 is said to have seriously degraded the combat readiness of U.S.-based ground units. Since the early 1960s the Army had counted on its reserve components to provide logistical and training support for any sizable operation. As a consequence, by 1966, Army units based in the United States "had been virtually stripped of logistical support and especially military construction units for Vietnam." In addition, while losing trained personnel for Vietnam, they had become "clogged" with trainees, while the reserves developed a backlog of more than 100,000 enlistees who needed training, all "because the Army had swelled beyond its capacity to train recruits without the federalization of reserve divisions for training purposes."[43]

In Europe, U.S. Army personnel were being drawn off by 1966 to support the activation of new units in the United States and the buildup in Vietnam.[44] In addition, during 1968, two-thirds of a mechanized division, one armored cavalry regiment, and other support units (with a

---

40. *Department of Defense Annual Report for Fiscal Year 1966*, pp. 30–31.
41. Weigley, *History of the United States Army*, p. 534.
42. Some sources indicate that the U.S. strategic reserve was down to five divisions at the start of 1968, because the 6th Infantry Division was never more than a paper unit. Data provided by U.S. Army Office of Military History.
43. Weigley, *History of the United States Army*, p. 534; *Department of Defense Annual Report for Fiscal Year 1967*, p. 145.
44. *Department of Defense Annual Report for Fiscal Year 1966*, p. 126.

combined personnel strength of about 28,000 men) were sent back from West Germany to the United States. This came in response to a number of developments: international balance-of-payments pressures, continuing Vietnam requirements, increased tensions in Korea, and serious domestic disturbances.[45] The units that came back remained formally assigned to Europe, however, and left their heavy equipment there. Since then, the United States has annually held a Reforger (return of forces to Germany) exercise in which the personnel from U.S.-based units fly to West Germany, draw their equipment, and participate in maneuvers.

While the state of America's unengaged active forces raised the importance of reserve readiness, the Johnson administration continued to push for efficiencies in reserve organization. For three successive years, however, Congress resisted administration attempts to merge the Guard and Reserve, cut 60,000 men from their combined strength, eliminate a number of units, and save about $150 million (in 1964 dollars) a year. Congress effectively blocked most of these proposals in 1967 by requiring that organized units be included in both the Guard and Reserve, and that *minimum* personnel strengths for both components be authorized annually by the armed services committees before funds were appropriated for pay and allowances. The administration believed that the Army reserve strengths authorized for fiscal 1968 exceeded the levels necessary to support its contingency plans.[46] In 1968, however, the administration did manage to complete part of its 1965 restructuring plan, thus leaving the Army's reserves in basically their current form. Again in hopes of raising readiness by concentrating available resources on fewer units, the six Reserve divisions and fifteen Guard divisions from the Reinforcing Reserve were eliminated along with other Reinforcing Reserve units. The administration saw no point in keeping these divisions since their low manning levels meant they would have taken twelve to eighteen months (the amount of time needed to raise new divisions) to achieve readiness. Although this reorganization made it possible to man practically all reserve units at 90 percent strength or

---

45. Ibid., *Fiscal Year 1968*, p. 147.
46. Martin Binkin, *U.S. Reserve Forces: The Problem of the Weekend Warrior* (Brookings Institution, 1974), p. 26. See also Binkin's discussion of the sources of domestic political support for the reserves and of the bureaucratic biases against them within the Defense Department (pp. 24–29).

higher, it appears that equipment shortages continued to constrain reserve readiness.[47]

By 1968, ten of America's twenty-three divisions were engaged in Southeast Asia, and the rest are said to have been suffering seriously from the loss of logistical support, personnel, and training capacity. The administration appears to have felt that it had no choice in refusing to mobilize for a limited war, fearing that political repercussions could have made it impossible to prosecute the war. Although skirmishes broke out in Korea during 1968, in Europe tension had remained at low ebb since the Berlin crisis subsided in 1962, and West Germany was continuing to make progress on its rearmament program. France's withdrawal from the NATO command structure in 1966, however, left questions in some minds about the viability of the flexible response strategy that NATO adopted in 1967. In addition, the Soviet invasion of Czechoslovakia in August 1968 was to become one source of growing concern about the military balance in Europe.

A One-and-a-Half-War Strategy, 1969–78

The nation had become deeply disillusioned with its struggle to contain communism in Southeast Asia and with all things military by the time the Nixon administration took office. Somewhat ironically, the culmination of long-standing Sino-Soviet differences in border clashes during 1969 finally dispelled the myth of monolithic communism. The new administration soon responded to these developments with three initiatives. First, pointing to the Sino-Soviet split and the failure of previous administrations to acquire the conventional forces believed needed for one minor and two major wars, the Nixon administration adopted a "one-and-a-half-war" strategy. Henceforth, the United States would "maintain in peacetime general purpose forces adequate for meeting a major communist attack in either Europe or Asia, assisting allies against non-Chinese threats in Asia, and contending with a [minor] contingency elsewhere."[48] Second, the Nixon administration advanced a doctrine

---

47. *Department of Defense Annual Report for Fiscal Year 1968*, pp. 40, 203, 205. By the end of 1970 the Army's reserve components had only $1.6 billion of the $6.1 billion worth of equipment required for mobilization. *Fiscal Year 1972–76 Defense Program and the 1972 Defense Budget* (GPO, 1971), p. 102.

48. Nixon, *U.S. Foreign Policy for the 1970s*, pp. 128–29.

for minimizing American involvement in any more "limited" wars in Asia. In cases of aggression not involving the Soviet Union or China, the United States would provide an ally with military and economic aid and, if necessary, air and naval support, but expect the directly threatened nation to provide the bulk of the manpower needed for its own defense.[49] This so-called Nixon doctrine, which reflected apparent national support for a lower American profile in Asia, provided a rationale for the reduction of U.S. ground forces in Vietnam and for the 1971 removal of one of two U.S. divisions from South Korea. It also set the stage for increased military sales and assistance by the United States to several Asian nations. Iran, the most notable among them, was expected to safeguard Western security interests in the Persian Gulf once Britain completed the withdrawal of its forces from the region in 1972. Third, the Nixon administration ended conscription in 1973, largely to assuage the antidraft sentiment aroused by the Vietnam War. For budgetary reasons and to enable them to meet all their manpower requirements through volunteer accessions, the administration also pared the active ground forces. By 1972, their personnel strength and number of divisions were, respectively, almost one-half and nearly one-third below 1968 levels. In announcing its initiatives, the administration emphasized its readiness to respond with nuclear weapons to a more demanding set of contingencies. Two former Defense Department officials have suggested that, inasmuch as the active forces had only three fewer divisions than in 1964 under the two-and-a-half-war strategy, the Nixon administration should have been more confident than its predecessors about the U.S. capacity for carrying out national strategy.[50]

Around 1974, U.S. military planning began to focus increasingly on Europe again. First, however, the Nixon administration had had to overcome congressional sentiment, led mainly by the Senate majority leader, Mike Mansfield, for cutting the U.S. ground presence in Europe by half. In military terms, the U.S. reemphasis on NATO made some sense. Removal of American forces during the Vietnam War, the 1968 introduction of five Soviet divisions into Czechoslovakia, and subse-

---

49. Arnold M. Kuzmack, "Foreign Policy and Military Force Planning," *Military Review*, vol. 52 (August 1972), pp. 19–20.

50. Leslie H. Gelb and Arnold M. Kuzmack suggested that a literal interpretation of the one-and-a-half-war strategy would have eliminated seven divisions. "General Purpose Forces," in Henry Owen, ed., *The Next Phase in Foreign Policy* (Brookings Institution, 1973), p. 208.

quent improvements in Soviet theater forces had produced an undesirable change in the balance of conventional forces. And improvements in the Soviet Union's nuclear forces were continuing to erode Western confidence in the credibility of its nuclear deterrent. Most observers would admit, however, that the conventional balance in Europe throughout the 1970s never came to seem as grim for NATO as it had appeared during the 1950s. Moreover, improvements in the political situation in Europe—evident in West Germany's *Ostpolitik,* the four-power agreement on Berlin's status, negotiations on mutual and balanced force reductions, and the Conference on Security and Cooperation in Europe—made the chances of war seem more remote than ever. All this suggests that the U.S. reemphasis on NATO may, in part, have stemmed from force of habit, disenchantment with the thought of limited contingencies elsewhere, and an assumption that the European balance provides an appropriate yardstick for sizing U.S. forces.[51]

This resurgence of interest in NATO resulted in the addition of three divisions and two brigades to the Army force structure during 1975 and 1976. The United States now had as many active divisions as it had maintained under the two-and-a-half-war strategy. The changes were prompted by concern that increases and improvements in Soviet forces in Eastern Europe after the Czechoslovakian crisis might enable the Soviet Union to launch an attack without substantial reinforcement or warning, as well as by analyses that highlighted apparent Soviet attachment to a short-war strategy designed to bring victory before NATO could mobilize its superior resources.[52] Maintaining that National Guard divisions could not respond on short warning and that the Army contained more logistical support than necessary for a short war,[53] the Ford

---

51. Secretary of Defense Harold Brown claimed that "if we have reasonable confidence of halting [a hypothetical Warsaw Pact attack in central Europe], it would be logical to assume that we have the basic forces to deal with other contingencies of a less demanding nature." *Department of Defense Annual Report, Fiscal Year 1979,* p. 87.

52. *Annual Defense Department Report, FY1976 and FY197T,* pp. III/14, III/41. For an unofficial but representative treatment of this matter, see Richard D. Lawrence and Jeffrey Record, *U.S. Force Structure in NATO: An Alternative* (Brookings Institution, 1974), pp. 6–26.

53. *Annual Defense Department Report, FY1976 and FY197T,* p. III/14. In supporting the first argument, Secretary of Defense James Schlesinger recalled that "it took a minimum of eleven months to ready [National Guard] divisions for combat in World War II and Korea." This is, however, an unfair statement. In both cases, low personnel and equipment levels before mobilization were largely to blame for low readiness.

administration encouraged the Army to give up support units and overhead to provide some of the personnel for the three new divisions. Additional personnel requirements were to be met through the use of one reserve brigade to round out each of four active divisions, including the three new ones. Creation of the two additional brigades for deployment in Europe stemmed from congressional insistence that 18,000 personnel spaces be converted from support to combat roles. Accommodated within existing active manpower levels, these changes again raised the Army's reliance on reserve components for support in any sizable military operation. In addition, the Ford and Carter administrations further mechanized the active Army. Lastly, in 1978 the Carter administration, mindful of a short-warning threat, began moving to preposition equipment in West Germany for four more U.S.-based divisions by 1982.

Ground capabilities for conflicts outside Europe received relatively little attention during this period, although the United States did retain active forces earmarked for a minor contingency. The disbandment of Strike Command in 1972 reflected official aversion toward military intervention.[54] For most of this period, a North Korean attack supported by the Soviet Union or China served as the most demanding minor contingency for force planning purposes. Given Soviet-American détente, continuing enmity between the Soviet Union and China, and growing rapprochement between the United States and China, it is reasonable to believe that this contingency was not taken very seriously.[55] Indeed, positive developments in Northeast Asia and a desire to free more forces for NATO led the Carter administration, in early 1977, to announce that the remaining U.S. division in South Korea would be withdrawn by 1982.[56] The withdrawal was indefinitely postponed, however, in response to the concerns of allies and an intelligence

---

54. It was replaced by the austerely manned Readiness Command, which had the more general mission of preparing forces for any contingency outside NATO.

55. For instance, the desirability of maintaining a U.S. strongpoint in Northeast Asia to prevent the movement of Soviet forces from the Far East to Europe in the event of a war there was one justification that Secretary Schlesinger offered for the continued presence of a U.S. Army division in South Korea. *Annual Defense Department Report, FY1976 and FY197T*, p. III/30.

56. Secretary of Defense Brown cited "our own need for greater flexibility in the allocation of our limited number of divisions." *Department of Defense Annual Report, Fiscal Year 1979*, p. 91. Since this division was to be "heavied up," he was presumably referring to a desire to earmark it for NATO.

reassessment that revealed the North Korean threat to be greater than had been thought.

The reserve components between 1968 and 1978 declined in strength by about 14 percent, largely because the elimination of conscription in 1973 removed a major incentive for reserve enlistment. Shortfalls became particularly pronounced in the Army National Guard and Reserve; by 1978 they had only about 75 percent of their war-required strength.[57] A final worrisome development was the sharp decline in the number of unpaid individual ready reservists that the Army could draw on for fillers or combat replacements. Without them, active or reserve units would probably have to be cannibalized to provide trained individuals for deploying units in the early stages of an operation. The major cause of this decline was the post-Vietnam drawdown, which decreased the number of individuals leaving active duty and entering the pool of ready reservists. By the late 1970s, shrinkage of the reservist pool had become a source of serious official concern. A number of congressmen and senior officers suggested drafting individual reservists—who would first spend a few months on active duty—as a means of enlarging the pool.

By 1978, it would have appeared to most observers that U.S. ground forces had largely recovered from the experience of Vietnam. Although the reserve components suffered from personnel and equipment shortages, that was nothing new. Much attention focused on the Ford-Carter initiatives to improve the U.S. ground posture vis-à-vis NATO, which were generally applauded. After 1973, however, there was growing concern about such things as Western access to Middle Eastern oil and Soviet adventurism in the third world. This concern would soon blossom, raising new questions about the role of U.S. ground forces in the defense of central Europe.

New Strains, Old Refrains

American ground force posture at the close of 1980 was still based on a one-and-a-half-war strategy, largely focused on the NATO mission. A Korean conflict had served as the minor contingency primarily used for planning purposes. Two Marine divisions were apparently earmarked as reinforcements for the one Army division stationed in South Korea.[58]

57. *Department of Defense Annual Report, Fiscal Year 1981*, p. 265.
58. Richard Burt, *New York Times*, January 6, 1978.

This left one Marine division, presumably oriented toward NATO's flanks, and fifteen Army divisions in the active force structure available for Europe. A number of divisions and separate brigades were also retained in the Army's reserve components for possible use on NATO's central front.[59] The Army's support structure—a less noticeable asset than its division "flags"—was also shaped with a short-warning, short war in Europe in mind. The many personnel spaces it converted from support to combat roles during the mid-1970s increased the Army's dependence on its reserve component for support in any sizable military operation.

By the end of 1980, however, a great deal of concern had developed over the possibility of a contingency in Southwest Asia. There was growing anxiety about Western access to Persian Gulf oil; the replacement of a friendly regime with revolutionary chaos in Iran; Soviet intervention capabilities; and Soviet activism in the region, which culminated in the invasion of Afghanistan; as well as other instances of regional instability, such as the Iran-Iraq war. The Carter administration responded with organizational and logistical initiatives. It established a joint task force in 1979 to prepare selected units for use as a rapid-deployment force. This force would be drawn from a reservoir of designated units and tailored to a particular contingency. In terms reminiscent of the early 1960s, it was expected that these deployments "could be anywhere from a platoon of rangers . . . to a multi-division corps."[60] The administration also embarked on a program (similarly reminiscent of the early 1960s) to procure maritime prepositioning ships, which would anchor at remote bases and hold the equipment and supplies for three Marine brigades. Seven leased ships containing materiel for a Marine brigade of 10,000–12,000 men were deployed to the Indian Ocean in the summer of 1980. It also negotiated for access to facilities in the region. Finally, the administration obtained legislation raising from 50,000 to 100,000 the number of reservists it could call up in an emergency

---

59. The Army's reserve components included 1 mechanized and 2 armored divisions, 4 armored cavalry regiments, and 7 mechanized and 3 armored brigades probably oriented toward NATO, and 5 infantry divisions and 10 separate infantry brigades that might also have been available. The Marine Corps Reserve had 1 division that might have been available as well.

60. *Department of Defense Annual Report, Fiscal Year 1981*, p. 116. The major ground units apparently in the pool included 1 corps and 1 mechanized, 1 airborne, and 1 air-mobile division from the Army, and 3 Marine brigades. See Drew Middleton, *New York Times*, March 20, 1980.

on its own authority. The first commander of the rapid-deployment force claimed that up to 100,000 reservists, most of whom would presumably come from the Army National Guard or Reserve, would be needed to support a corps-sized deployment to the Persian Gulf because of the force structure changes made during the mid-1970s.[61] The Army was once more forced to look to the reserve components for support for any substantial operation, mainly because the active forces had traded support units for NATO-oriented combat units. Although the Carter administration considered adding another active Army division,[62] it finally decided that its other initiatives were adequate.

Some observers, however, were concerned about the ability of U.S. ground forces to meet contingencies in Europe *and* in other regions. Historians could question the rapid-deployment force's reliance on limited mobilization of reservists, a situation caused largely by force structure adaptations to the threat of a short, surprise war in Europe. After all, the limited mobilizations for Korea and Berlin had encountered numerous difficulties, while the failure to mobilize for Vietnam—presumably to avoid problems with reservists, their state governments, and their congressmen—caused the unengaged portion of U.S. ground forces to lose their logistical support, to become clogged with trainees, and to lose trained personnel to the war effort. But the United States has sacrificed limited war capabilities for general war capabilities in the past, most notably between 1945 and 1950. A more obvious source of concern is the possibility of more than one and a half simultaneous contingencies, something pointed to by William Kaufmann, a consultant to several secretaries of defense.[63] Although military planners appear to posit a requirement of four divisions to meet a contingency in the Persian Gulf,[64] America has not created any additional active ground forces since it accepted responsibility for that region's security. It does appear that the Army's one airborne division, at least, was removed from the list of forces earmarked for Europe in order to leave it available for other contingencies. Maintaining that the world became a more turbulent place during the 1970s, Kaufmann suggests that the United States might be

61. John J. Fialka, *Washington Star*, June 19, 1980.
62. Benjamin F. Schemmer, "Army Loses 17th Active Division Sought for New Rapid Reaction Force," *Armed Forces Journal International*, vol. 117 (January 1980), p. 14.
63. William W. Kaufmann, "The Defense Budget," in Joseph A. Pechman, ed., *Setting National Priorities: The 1982 Budget* (Brookings Institution, 1981), pp. 161–62.
64. Richard Burt, *New York Times*, January 6, 1978.

confronted by several more or less simultaneous contingencies—in Europe, Northeast or Southwest Asia, or Latin America—and might then have to allocate a deficit of four or so divisions between Europe and other regions.

The readiness of the reserve components to support either a major or a minor contingency continues to be constrained by equipment and personnel shortages. The 1980 dollar value of equipment for the National Guard, which contains the bulk of organized reserve units, remained at only 69 percent of the total wartime requirement.[65] As of 1980, the paid-drill strength of the Army National Guard and Reserve was still only about 75 percent of the total needed to bring all units to wartime strength.[66] There also remained a serious shortage of unpaid, individual reservists. Because of personnel shortfalls in reserve component units and low levels of individual reservists, it appears that the Army would have only 84 percent of the personnel needed to man all its active and reserve units ninety days after the start of a full mobilization. The Army fears that forward-deployed and early deploying units would have to fight at less than wartime strengths, and that later deploying units and the U.S. base structure would have to be stripped of trained personnel to replace casualties and fill early deploying units.[67] Although the reserve components were in better shape than they were in 1950, even a limited mobilization would encounter problems similar to those experienced in the 1961 mobilization over Berlin.

All this immediately raises two important questions. First, given the appearance of new demands in Southwest Asia, what active forces should the United States continue to earmark for NATO? Second, what role might the reserve components reasonably be expected to play?

65. Maj. Gen. Emmett H. Walker, Jr., USA, "Progress in Training, Readiness, Manning," *Army*, vol. 30 (October 1980), p. 152.
66. International Institute for Strategic Studies, *The Military Balance, 1980–1981* (London: IISS, 1980), p. 7; *Department of Defense Annual Report, Fiscal Year 1980*, p. 279.
67. Maj. Gen. William R. Berkman, USA, "Reserves: Expanded Missions, Limited Resources," *Army*, vol. 30 (October 1980), p. 168; information provided by the Department of the Army.

CHAPTER THREE

DEMANDS ON GROUND FORCES IN CENTRAL EUROPE IN THE 1980s

It is impossible to forecast how successful NATO's conventional forces would be at waging a forward defense of the central front, a goal dictated largely by geographical considerations. The military equation in central Europe involves just too much complexity and uncertainty. It is reasonable, however, to gauge the degree of confidence that NATO could justifiably feel today, while at peace, regarding its defensive prospects.

In this chapter, current Western capabilities are measured against several standards for assessing the more readily quantifiable aspects of the ground force equation. From these comparisons it appears that NATO should feel something more than low confidence but something less than high confidence in its defensive capacity. It also appears that any shortfalls in the planned deployment of its ground forces would be more likely to arise later rather than earlier in NATO's mobilization. The picture could be dramatically changed, however, by such eventualities as an Eastern European country's refusal to take part in an attack or unexpected demands on U.S. forces in other parts of the world. Those possibilities aside, the projections in this chapter indicate that in many cases the numerical balance of ground forces would not clearly favor either side. In those circumstances, a conflict could turn on such factors as the extent of terrain preparation, readiness, logistics, command and control, and air power; NATO might enjoy a slight lead in some of these matters.

NATO's Central Front

The central front of NATO roughly corresponds with West Germany's eastern border, which is about 885 kilometers long. About 800 kilometers of this border are under Allied Forces Central Europe (AFCENT), a

NATO command that encompasses Belgium, the Netherlands, and most of West Germany. Along with Denmark and Norway, West Germany north of the Elbe River (about 85 kilometers of which border East Germany) is formally part of Allied Forces Northern Europe (AF-NORTH). This arrangement is somewhat artificial. For the purposes of this study, all of West Germany is regarded as being part of NATO's central region.

The lack of depth in the region discourages plans for wide-ranging defensive maneuvers of the kind the Germans executed in Russia during World War II.[1] From the East German border, it is less than 40 kilometers to the outskirts of Hamburg, about 150 kilometers to the fringes of the Rhine-Ruhr industrial conurbation (Dortmund), and about 100 kilometers to Frankfurt, the site of large U.S. military depots. About 30 percent of West Germany's population and 25 percent of its industrial capacity lie within 100 kilometers of the East German border.

Not surprisingly, the West German government insists that there can be no alternative to forward defense, which it defines as "a coherent defence conducted close to the intra-German border with the aim of losing as little ground as possible and confining damage to a minimum. This includes the recapture of lost territory."[2] A strategy of forward defense of course carries with it the risk of penetration and encirclement; yet any serious move to deemphasize forward defense would cause severe political strains within the alliance.[3]

The "intra-German border" that must be defended could reasonably be defined as a 750-kilometer perimeter running by or through Lübeck, Lüneburg, Braunschweig, Göttingen, Fulda, Bayreuth, and Freyung. West German forces, probably with Danish assistance, would defend the line north of the Elbe River (about 70 kilometers). The 680-kilometer

1. Von Manstein's defense along the Donets River in March–April 1943 was a classic example of mobile defense. One author superimposes this campaign on a map of West Germany to help make the point that "free-wheeling, mobile defense operations require more space than the NATO center can afford." Gen. William E. Depuy, USA ret., "Technology and Tactics in Defense of Europe," *Army*, vol. 29 (April 1979), pp. 20–21.

2. West German Minister of Defense, *White Paper 1979: The Security of the Federal Republic of Germany and the Development of the Federal Armed Forces* (Federal Minister of Defense, 1979), p. 126.

3. In 1977, Washington got a taste of what would happen, after press reports suggested that the Carter administration was contemplating the option of conceding one-third of West Germany in the event of attack. See Rowland Evans and Robert Novak, *Washington Post*, August 4, 1977; Edward Walsh, *Washington Post*, August 4, 1977.

Figure 3-1. Corps Sectors of Military Responsibility on NATO's Central Front

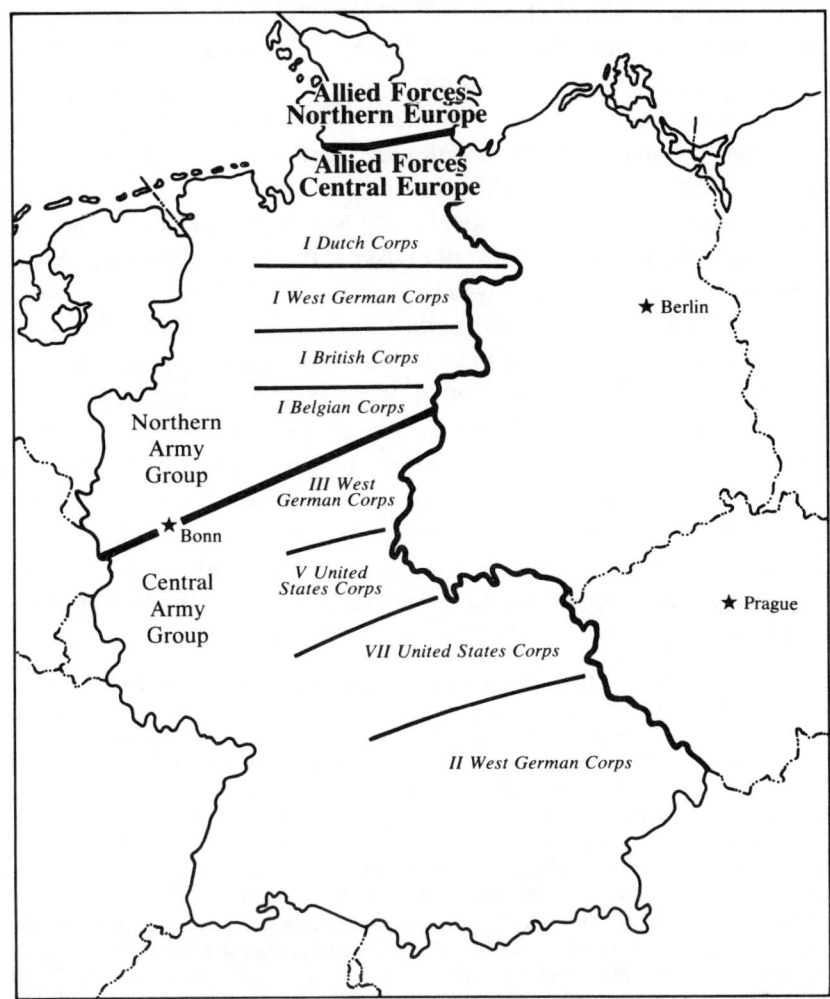

Sources: Congressional Budget Office, *U.S. Ground Forces: Design and Cost Alternatives for NATO and Non-NATO Contingencies,* prepared by Pat Hillier and Nora Slatkin (CBO, 1980), p. 11; and *Aviation Week and Space Technology,* June 7, 1982, p. 57.

portion under the command of AFCENT is divided, "layer cake" fashion, into eight corps sectors (see figure 3-1). The deployment of forces from five different nations at the border is believed to strengthen deterrence.[4] Bolstering these corps are a French corps (not formally at

4. See Gen. Ulrich de Maiziere, GA (ret.), "Rational Deployment of Forces on the Central Front," study prepared for the Assembly of the Western European Union, April 2, 1975, p. 38.

NATO's disposal) and a Canadian brigade located in the rear. The corps in the Northern Army Group (NORTHAG) would offer an attacker closer proximity than those in the Central Army Group (CENTAG) to strategic objectives along the Rhine.

The region's terrain varies considerably. While the roads throughout are of high quality, only those within the sectors of the I British Corps, III West German Corps, V U.S. Corps, and VII U.S. Corps are thought to present good east-west connections.[5] North of the Harz Mountains, in the sectors controlled by NORTHAG, "the land is generally flat or gently rolling and is crisscrossed by numerous small water obstacles." The border areas in the sectors controlled by CENTAG are, except for a few corridors like the one near Fulda, rugged and heavily wooded.[6] Forests cover about 29 percent of West Germany, and government afforestation programs are increasing the proportion slightly each year.[7] Another 9 percent of the land is built up; urban sprawl, like that around Hamburg, Hannover, and Kassel in the border areas, and the Rhine-Ruhr conurbation to the west, is expected to increase during the 1980s.[8] Villages abound; on average, every twelve square kilometers contain a village of less than three thousand inhabitants[9]—hence the U.S. Army's assumption that "combat in Germany will automatically involve re-

---

5. According to one U.S. Defense Department consultant, the existence there of parallel roads and terrain suitable for movement of armor would facilitate the maneuver of armored units. Elsewhere, he maintains, the armor would be vulnerable to ambush or long-range antitank fire. Steven L. Canby, *Short (And Long) War Responses: Restructuring, Border Defense, and Reserve Mobilization for Armored Warfare*, prepared for U.S. Department of Defense, Director of Special Studies (Santa Monica, Calif.: Technology Service Corp., 1978), pp. 52–53. It appears that off-road movement by armor could be particularly difficult in the I Dutch Corps and I West German Corps sectors, which are dominated by the boggy Lüneburg heath. According to a former commander of the U.S. Army in Europe, "in particularly wet weather, fairly common in this area, almost all travel is road-bound; cross-country transit can be said to be good only in the dead of winter when the terrain is frozen hard." Gen. James H. Polk, USA (ret.), "The North German Plain Attack Scenario: Threat or Illusion," *Strategic Review*, vol. 8 (Summer 1980), p. 62.

6. Richard D. Lawrence and Jeffrey Record, *U.S. Force Structure in NATO: An Alternative* (Brookings Institution, 1974), pp. 28–29. Most observers agree with their assessment that—for reasons of proximity and terrain—the CENTAG area is "more favorable to the defense than NORTHAG."

7. Information provided by the West German embassy in Washington. Forested area has increased by about 0.8 percent per year. Paul Bracken, "Urban Sprawl and NATO Defense," *Survival*, vol. 18 (November–December 1976), p. 257.

8. Canby, *Short (And Long) War Responses*, p. 51; Bracken, "Urban Sprawl and NATO Defense," pp. 255–57.

9. Canby, *Short (And Long) War Responses*, p. 53.

peated, almost continuous battle for cities, towns, villages, and adjacent built-up areas."[10]

The nature of West Germany's terrain, and ongoing changes in it, have raised questions about NATO's strategy of flexible response and the structure of its conventional forces. Urbanization and afforestation have engendered debate over the utility of light forces in the region. Since the early 1960s, the predominant view has been that only heavy (armored or mechanized infantry) forces are suitable for use in central Europe. But Canby argues that the natural terrain in up to two-thirds of the AFCENT border region could accommodate light infantry and that every corps sector contains militarily significant built-up areas that light forces could defend.[11] Two senior West German officers, one of whom argues that heavy forces are unsuited for about 50 percent of the Federal Republic's terrain, have criticized Bonn for neglecting light infantry. The inspector of the West German Army has replied that mountains reduce the area available for operations, leaving only 24 percent of the relevant terrain suitable for light infantry; he would welcome an increase in light infantry, but not at the expense of mechanized forces.[12] The U.S. Army's chief of staff sees a need now to "continually examine the utility of light, rapidly deployable divisions in Central Europe to achieve a balance of heavy and light forces that will provide a better overall defense posture given the terrain variations and urban sprawl that exists and is projected in much of the region."[13]

Ground Force Requirements

While he was secretary of defense, James R. Schlesinger stated that the ground force requirement for most contingencies depends on three factors. "The first is the ratio of force to space. Whether we are talking

10. U.S. Department of the Army, *Operations,* FM100-5 (1976), p. 13/16.
11. *Short (And Long) War Responses,* pp. 51–54.
12. For a report on this West German debate, see Udo Philipp, "NATO Strategy Under Discussion in Bonn," *International Defense Review,* vol. 13, no. 9 (1980), pp. 1367–71. The West German Army recently moved to add two battalions of motorized infantry to each of its eleven regular divisions. West German Minister of Defense, *White Paper 1979,* pp. 152–54. West Germany's Field Army would not normally deploy light infantry units larger than a battalion in forward areas.
13. Gen. Edward C. Meyer, USA, *White Paper 1980: A Framework for Molding the Army of the 1980s into a Disciplined, Well-Trained Fighting Force* (U.S. Government Printing Office, 1980), p. 3.

about Central Europe or Korea, if a front is to be held along its length with a reasonable degree of confidence, there must be a minimum density of manpower along that front, with no significant gaps between units." The second is a requirement for operational reserves, "both locally and at higher levels, that can be allocated to halt penetrations or develop counterattacks." The third is the ratio of forces, which "should not be allowed to favor an attacker by too great a margin."[14]

Force-to-Space Requirements

The significance of force-to-space ratios repeatedly impressed military historian B. H. Liddell Hart. He noted that once the ratio of defenders to the amount of space being defended reaches some threshold, an attacking force—despite a numerical superiority of 5:1 or even higher—can well find it impossible to move rapidly through that defense.[15] The defense may eventually be worn down and pushed back; but, in the meantime, it can perhaps hold up the offense long enough for defender reinforcements to arrive or for counterattacks to get under way. The Soviet military appears to be similarly impressed; it has long held that a defense's force-to-space ratio has a critical effect on the offense's rate of advance.[16]

Force-to-space requirements for a defense force depend in part on terrain and on the quality of equipment, training, and leadership. But firepower and mobility clearly are judged the principal determinants of force-to-space requirements. As firepower and mobility have increased, division frontages have expanded. Whereas fifteen kilometers was considered the normal defensive frontage for an American infantry division during World War II,[17] some Army officers now suggest that a

---

14. *Annual Defense Department Report, FY1976 and FY197T*, p. III/15.
15. B. H. Liddell Hart, *Deterrent or Defense: A Fresh Look at the West's Military Position* (Praeger, 1960), pp. 97–109.
16. Phillip A. Karber, "The Soviet Anti-Tank Debate," *Survival*, vol. 18 (May–June 1976), p. 111.
17. Liddell Hart charts the decline in force-to-space requirements since Napoleon. See *Deterrent or Defense*, pp. 97–109; see also U.S. Army Training and Doctrine Command, *Division Restructuring Study: Phase I Report* (Fort Monroe, Va.: USA-TRADOC, 1977), vol. 1, pp. 2–3; Hugh M. Cole, *The Ardennes: Battle of the Bulge* (GPO, 1965), p. 56. The Battle of the Bulge suggests that a defensive frontage of 15 kilometers was a good rule of thumb. The German advance in that 1944 battle stopped when the average density of the opposing U.S. line climbed to one division every 16 kilometers. See Cole, *The Ardennes*, p. 651.

heavy U.S. division could defend a front of anywhere from thirty to sixty kilometers.[18]

For planning purposes, analysts in the Office of the Secretary of Defense posit twenty-five kilometers as a standard frontage for a U.S. heavy division in central Europe.[19] Divisions might, if necessary, hold wider fronts. But force ratios would then shift to the attacker's advantage; apart from that, a widening of frontage would increase the amount of territory to be covered by the defender's artillery and could decrease the direct-fire support that combat units could provide each other. At some point, the defense would be stretched so thin that a breakthrough could occur.

Operational Reserves

Operational reserves are used to halt penetrations before they turn into breakthroughs and to develop counterattacks. Some general rules of thumb exist for sizing operational reserves. Liddell Hart suggested that half of any defense's forces should be held in operational reserve, "even where it entails thinning the forward defence to a hazardous degree."[20] This is a fairly extreme position.

Currently, NATO follows another standard on its central front. The size of operational reserves at each echelon appears to be two levels below that echelon: a corps for the theater, a division for each army group, a brigade for each corps, and so on. By this formula, roughly one-quarter (including five divisions held at levels above corps) of the forces deployed by NATO after two or so weeks of mobilization are intended to function as operational reserves. The corps designated as AFCENT's operational reserve would, however, have to come from the United States.

There is a good deal of concern about this state of affairs. Secretary of Defense Harold Brown maintained that one of NATO's most serious problems was the shortage of operational reserves, especially in the

18. See Lt. Col. Donald B. Vought, USA (ret.), and Lt. Col. J. R. Angolia, USA, "The United States Army," in Ray Bonds, ed., *The U.S. War Machine* (Crown, 1978), p. 74; USATRADOC, *Division Restructuring Study*, p. 3. These ranges probably are based on assessments of minimal requirements rather than optimal deployment patterns.

19. Interview. The norm would be wider in mountainous regions, narrower in forested or urban areas, and narrower for traditional infantry divisions.

20. B. H. Liddell Hart, "Shield Forces for NATO," *Survival*, vol. 2 (May–June 1960), p. 110.

event of an attack preceded by little advance preparation.[21] Canby has long argued that a lack of adequate operational reserves is NATO's greatest deficiency. He suggests expanding NATO's operational reserves to contain from six to twenty-four divisions, depending on the strength of its forward defenses. On average, Canby seems to suggest that one-third of NATO's forces be withheld as operational reserves.[22]

Force Ratios

In ground combat, more forces are normally needed to attack than to defend. Hence, military equations are sometimes viewed in terms of "threshold" ratios. In theory, any attack is likely to fail unless the ratio of attacker to defender forces reaches a certain threshold.[23] Harold Brown has held that a ratio of 2:1, "while certainly not ensuring ultimate victory" for the Warsaw Pact, "could be decisive in determining the outcome of the early battles" and "could enable the Pact to gain breakthroughs that, if unchecked, could permit further rapid advances into NATO territory."[24] Secretary Schlesinger, however, felt that "if an attacker could achieve a favorable overall ratio of perhaps 1.5:1 in several . . . respects, he could embark on such large local concentrations that the defender would find it difficult to prevent one or more breakthroughs."[25] Two analysts in the Congressional Budget Office suggest that if the ratio were kept below 1.4:1, NATO could conduct an "elastic" defense, whereby a continuous line would be maintained while territory was traded for mobilization time; while if the ratio were 1.2:1, NATO could wage a "steadfast" defense, whereby an attack would be held at the border.[26]

21. *Department of Defense Annual Report, Fiscal Year 1981*, p. 48.
22. He suggests that if NATO's central front had a forward defense of about 42 divisions, only 6 would be needed as operational reserves, while if it had an operational reserve of 24 divisions, NATO would need only about 20 divisions at the front. *Short (And Long) War Responses*, pp. 80–92. (He does not explain how he derived these figures.)
23. A three-to-one rule is most commonly cited; however, it is really meant to apply to division-sized engagements or smaller. Congressional Budget Office (CBO), *Assessing the NATO/Warsaw Pact Military Balance*, prepared by James Blaker and Andrew Hamilton (GPO, 1977), pp. 59–61.
24. *Department of Defense Annual Report, Fiscal Year 1982*, p. 74.
25. *Annual Defense Department Report, FY1976 and FY197T*, p. III/15.
26. CBO, *U.S. Ground Forces: Design and Cost Alternatives for NATO and Non-NATO Contingencies*, prepared by Pat Hillier and Nora Slatkin (CBO, 1980), pp. 8, 16–18.

There are limits to the utility of such static analysis. Many unrepresented factors would also affect the outcome of a conflict. Indeed, some studies indicate that, historically, the results of battles have been relatively insensitive to prevailing force ratios.[27] Hence, force ratios cannot reasonably be used to do more than establish probabilities.

Force ratios can be derived from any number of static indicators. Some are regarded as more useful than others (see appendix A). In this chapter, force ratios are based on manpower in major combat units. The manpower counts here are divided by the personnel strength of a standard U.S. armored division (18,300 men) to produce a manpower division equivalent.

A Composite Approach

The three indexes of force strength that Secretary Schlesinger advocated can imply quite different force requirements for NATO. For instance, to meet the Defense Department's desire to assign a division nothing wider than a 25-kilometer front, NATO would need thirty divisions to cover its 750-kilometer central front. If, however, NATO intends to hold one-third of its force as an operational reserve, it would need forty-five divisions. And if NATO wishes to maintain a 1.5:1 ratio of offensive to defensive forces, it would need fifty-three divisions to counter an enemy force equivalent to eighty divisions.

It is reasonable to expect that the relative importance of force-to-space ratios, operational reserves, and force ratios would depend on the extent of mobilization and reinforcement or, more important, the stage of fighting at hand. Early in any buildup, NATO's requirements would be driven by the need to cover the central front on defensible frontages—that is, to achieve reasonable force-to-space ratios. Subsequently, at the onset of fighting, initial operational reserves would be needed to contain penetrations and permit an aggressive forward defense. If these needs were met, force ratios during these early stages would be a secondary consideration. The ratio of forces would become important, however,

---

27. A U.S. Army analysis of 1,000 tank battles suggested, for instance, that force ratios have very little impact on outcomes. Gen. Donn A. Starry, USA, "A Tactical Evolution—FM100-5," *Military Review*, vol. 58 (August 1978), pp. 6–7. Two other analysts argue that training and tactics are the dominant aspects of combat capability. See Jack N. Merritt and Pierre M. Sprey, "Negative Marginal Returns in Weapons Acquisition," in Richard G. Head and Ervin J. Rokke, eds., *American Defense Policy*, 3d ed. (Johns Hopkins University Press, 1973), pp. 491–92.

as the full Warsaw Pact force is brought to bear, as the front line expands with enemy penetrations, and as NATO forces suffer losses. Then, the relative numbers of its forces would become the major determinant of the confidence NATO could have toward defending the central front.

Warsaw Pact Forces

The Soviet approach to theater warfare, it is generally agreed, is wholly offensive in its operational orientation. Indeed, Soviet writers maintain that only offensive operations can produce victory.[28] Statements about the need for decisive attacks, carried out to great depth and aimed at the total defeat of enemy defenders and the capture of vital areas of enemy territory, have led most Western observers to conclude that domination of central Europe, perhaps including France, would be the goal of any Warsaw Pact attack.[29] Calls for continuous operations and high rates of advance indicate that Moscow favors a speedy resolution of any conflict,[30] before NATO's superior resources could be mobilized and brought to bear, or before the West could reach a decision to use nuclear weapons.[31] Warsaw Pact armies have forgone the support units thought necessary for prolonged operations and thus can field more combat units and more combat power than Western armies, given the same level of manpower and equipment.[32] In addition, most Western analysts expect that the Warsaw Pact would attempt to concentrate much of its combat power—ground formations in a conventional conflict,

---

28. For example, see V. Ye. Savkin, *The Basic Principles of Operational Art and Tactics,* trans. under U.S. Air Force auspices (GPO, 1972), p. 242.

29. For example, see ibid., p. 255. Some analysts suggest, however, that despite the seeming irrationality of a "quick grab," a limited offensive might adequately serve Soviet purposes if it could hobble West Germany, break up NATO, and demoralize the West while avoiding nuclear escalation, and that, hence, this strategic option cannot be dismissed out of hand. For instance, see Richard K. Betts, *Surprise Attack: Lessons for Defense Planning* (Brookings Institution, 1982), p. 218.

30. For example, see Savkin, *Basic Principles,* pp. 167–74; A. A. Sidorenko, *The Offensive,* trans. under U.S. Air Force auspices (GPO, 1970), p. 200–20.

31. The population of NATO is about 570 million while that of the Warsaw Pact is only about 370 million; NATO's GNP is about $4 trillion, the Warsaw Pact's about $1.4 trillion. *Department of State Bulletin,* vol. 79 (April 1979), p. 3. As regards the Soviet view on nuclear escalation, see C. N. Donnelly, "Tactical Problems Facing the Soviet Army: Recent Debates in the Soviet Military Press," *International Defense Review,* vol. 11, no. 9 (1978), p. 1405.

32. Many American analysts have discussed this. For example, see Robert Lucas Fischer, *Defending the Central Front: The Balance of Forces,* Adelphi Paper 127 (London: International Institute for Strategic Studies, 1976), pp. 11–14; Lawrence and

or nuclear fires in a nuclear one—on a few key points in order to break through opposing defenses and precipitate their wholesale collapse.[33] And it is assumed that as a means of multiplying the operational impact of its combat power, the Warsaw Pact would pursue surprise—strategic, operational, and tactical.[34] (One analyst warns that improvements in NATO's antitank capabilities have heightened Moscow's interest in achieving strategic surprise through a preemptive offensive.)[35]

The Warsaw Pact states have the equivalent of about two hundred and thirty-one divisions, which are listed in table 3-1. In theory, three to five divisions would be attached to an army and about five armies would be assigned to a front, which roughly corresponds to a Western army group. Armies and fronts would also command combat support and service support units.[36] Because many Warsaw Pact divisions are

---

Record, *U.S. Force Structure*, pp. 13–16; Steven Canby, *The Alliance and Europe*, pt. 4: *Military Doctrine and Technology*, Adelphi Paper 109 (London: IISS, 1975), pp. 9–11.

33. Warsaw Pact ground forces are expected to mass in waves, or echelons. At any particular level of organization, it appears that roughly two-thirds of the breakthrough force would be in the first echelon and the remaining one-third in the second; "Soviet Army Echelonment and Objectives," prepared for the Centag Commanders Conference (Defense Nuclear Agency, 1978), p. 2. One analyst suggests, however, that Warsaw Pact forces would not bother to echelon if strategic surprise over NATO could be achieved. P. H. Vigor, "Soviet Army Wave Attack Philosophy: The Single-Echelon Option," *International Defense Review*, vol. 12, no. 1 (1979).

34. For a typical Soviet appraisal of the value of surprise, see Savkin, *Basic Principles*, pp. 231–33. In Soviet parlance, "the attacker's success in concealing his intent and timing yields strategic surprise; misdirecting the opponent's calculations of the time, strength, direction, speed, and manner of possible attacks generates operational surprise; and tactical surprise derives from the unexpected weapons, techniques, and skills that are actually employed in combat." John Despres, Lilita Dzirkals, and Barton Whaley, *Timely Lessons of History: The Manchurian Model for Soviet Strategy*, R-1825-NA, prepared for Office of the Secretary of Defense/Director of Net Assessment (Santa Monica, Calif.: Rand Corp., 1976), p. 16.

35. Karber, "Soviet Anti-Tank Debate," pp. 110–11.

36. Fronts would become operational only in wartime. It is believed that the headquarters of military districts in the border areas of the Soviet Union and the headquarters of groups of Soviet forces stationed outside the Soviet Union would form the nuclei of fronts. A front has no set size or organization. Although many organizational structures are possible, a typical front might contain about five armies, possibly an airborne division, one or more artillery divisions, one or more surface-to-surface missile brigades, several air defense brigades, and communications, engineering, transport, and other support units. In addition to three to five divisions, an army might typically contain an artillery brigade and the other support units a front might have, but usually of battalion rather than brigade size. U.S. Department of the Army, Office of the Assistant Chief of Staff for Intelligence, *Military Operations of the Soviet Army*, USAITAD report 14-U-76 (Department of the Army, 1976), pp. 79–81, 90–92, 98.

Table 3-1. Warsaw Pact Deployments, 1980

National army	Number of division-equivalents[a]			
	Armored	Mechanized	Airborne	Total
Bulgaria	1⅔	8	0	9⅔
Czechoslovakia	5	5	⅓	10⅓
East Germany	2	4	0	6
Hungary	1	5	0	6
Poland	5	8	2[b]	15
Romania	2	9	⅓	11⅓
Soviet Union[c]				
Czechoslovakia	2	3	0	5
East Germany	9	10	0	19
Hungary	2	2	0	4
Poland	2	0	0	2
Baltic MD	3	5	2	10
Belorussian MD	9	2	1	12
Carpathian MD	2	9	0	11
Kiev MD	7	4	0	11
Odessa MD	0	6	1	7
Leningrad MD	0	8	1	9
Moscow MD	2	4	1	7
Ural MD	1	2	0	3
Volga MD	0	3	0	3
North Caucasus MD	1	5	0	6
Transcaucasus MD	0	11	1	12
Turkestan MD	0	5	1	6
Central Asian MD	1	6	0	7
Siberian MD	0	5	0	5
Transbaykal MD	3	7	0	10
Far Eastern MD	1	20	0	21
Mongolia	1	2	0	3
Total	62⅔	158	10⅔	231⅓

Source: International Institute for Strategic Studies, *The Military Balance, 1980–1981* (London: IISS, 1980), pp. 10–11, 15–17.
a. Assumes that 3 brigades or regiments equal 1 division.
b. Includes 1 amphibious assault division.
c. Assignment of Soviet divisions, by country or by military district (MD) in the USSR. Figures include 6 or so Soviet divisions in Afghanistan.

normally manned much below their wartime strength, these armies get more divisions from a given active-duty personnel strength than Western armies do.

The Warsaw Pact armies have three readiness categories. In the Soviet Army, category 1 divisions are 75–100 percent manned and have all their equipment; category 2 are 50–75 percent manned and have all their fighting vehicles; and category 3 are about 25 percent manned and may be lacking some fighting vehicles and other equipment, and all of the equipment they have tends to be obsolete. In Eastern European armies, category 1 divisions are manned at no more than 75 percent strength, category 2 at up to 50 percent, and category 3 at perhaps 25 percent strength.[37] Table 3-2 gives a possible listing of the readiness category of selected Warsaw Pact divisions. Upon mobilization, understrength divisions would have to be filled out with reservists. Their readiness could strongly influence the amount of time the Warsaw Pact armies would need to mobilize and deploy their forces.[38]

No one knows what forces would participate in a Warsaw Pact attack, or how much preparation time would be required beforehand. For planning purposes, the U.S. Defense Department appears to focus on four possible contingencies: a two-front attack or a three-front attack by forces based in Eastern Europe, an attack reinforced from the three westernmost military districts of the Soviet Union, and an attack augmented by forces from additional Soviet military districts.[39] Preparation time would depend on the size of the attack. Understrength divisions would have to be filled out, fuel and ammunition distributed, units moved to wartime assembly areas, and command and logistical systems set up and shaken down. Some of this might well be done under the guise of exercises. Indeed, the idea of a clearly identifiable day that would mark the beginning of a Warsaw Pact mobilization might be misleading.[40] Uncertainties about all this have produced varying estimates of the time needed to prepare an attack.

37. International Institute for Strategic Studies, *The Military Balance, 1981–1982* (London: IISS, 1981), pp. 12, 18.

38. It is usually assumed that forward-deployed, full-strength Soviet divisions could move within a day of receiving orders. Fischer assumes that other, understrength category 1 divisions could be filled out by the third day of mobilization; *Defending the Central Front*, p. 20. Friedrich Wiener and William J. Lewis maintain that such units could deploy on 12–18 hours' notice, and that category 2 and perhaps many category 3 divisions could be ready to move within three days; *The Warsaw Pact Armies* (Vienna: Carl Ueberreuter, 1977), pp. 59–60. For sketchy evidence supporting the latter view, see *Allocation of Resources in the Soviet Union and China—1978*, Hearings before the Joint Economic Committee, 95 Cong. 2 sess. (GPO, 1978), pt. 4, p. 250. Jeffrey Record states that category 2 divisions are not believed deployable until 30 days after mobilization begins and category 3 not until 90 or even 120 days; *Sizing Up the Soviet Army* (Brookings Institution, 1975), pp. 21–22. A 1973 Defense Department study assumed it would take 12 weeks to fill out category 3 divisions; see Michael Getler, *Washington Post*, June 7, 1973.

39. *Department of Defense Annual Report, Fiscal Year 1980*, p. 101; Michael Getler, *Washington Post*, June 7, 1973; Richard Burt, *New York Times*, January 6, 1978.

40. Fischer, *Defending the Central Front*, pp. 15–17.

Table 3-2. Readiness of Warsaw Pact Divisions in Selected Regions, by Category, 1980

Region and national army	Number of category 1 divisions			Number of category 2 divisions			Number of category 3 divisions		
	Armored	Mechanized	Airborne	Armored	Mechanized	Airborne	Armored	Mechanized	Airborne
Eastern Europe	26	28	0	0	3	2⅓	2	6	0
Czechoslovakia	3	3	0	0	0	⅓	2	2	0
East Germany	2	4	0	0	0	0	0	0	0
Hungary	1	3	0	0	1	0	0	1	0
Poland	5	3	0	0	2	2[a]	0	3	0
Soviet Union[b]									
Czechoslovakia	2	3	0	0	0	0	0	0	0
East Germany	9	10	0	0	0	0	0	0	0
Hungary	2	2	0	0	0	0	0	0	0
Poland	2	0	0	0	0	0	0	0	0
Western Russia[c]	1	1	3	5	10	0	8	5	0
Baltic MD	0	0	2	1	3	0	2	2	0
Belorussian MD	0	1	1	3	1	0	6	0	0
Carpathian MD	1	0	0	1	6	0	0	3	0
Central Russia[c]	0	0	1	1	1	0	10	18	0
Kiev MD	0	0	0	0	0	0	7	4	0
Moscow MD	0	0	1	0	0	0	2	4	0
Ural MD	0	0	0	0	0	0	1	2	0
Volga MD	0	0	0	0	0	0	0	3	0
Central Asian MD	0	0	0	1	1	0	0	5	0
Total	27	29	4	6	14	2⅓	20	29	0

Source: IISS, *Military Balance, 1980–1981*, pp. 10–11, 15–17, 111.
a. Includes 1 amphibious assault division.
b. Assignment of Soviet divisions, by other country.
c. Assignment of Soviet divisions, by military district (MD).

A TWO-FRONT ATTACK. Presumably a two-front attack would be built around the Group of Soviet Forces in Germany (GSFG) and the Soviet Central Group of Forces (CGF) in Czechoslovakia. The GSFG is so important to Soviet military planning that it is the only group of Soviet forces abroad that has peacetime control over an artillery division, and its maneuver divisions are larger than other Soviet divisions. The East German Army would probably participate in any GSFG operation. It alone among Eastern European armies appears to have been given an essential role in Soviet war plans.[41]

A two-front attack would command about twenty-one divisions' worth of manpower in major combat units (see appendix B for the likely composition of this force). The time needed to organize such an attack has been estimated at as little as two days. Such estimates reflect the view put forward by Senators Nunn and Bartlett that the deployment of five Soviet divisions in Czechoslovakia and the subsequent augmentation and modernization of GSFG forces had given Moscow "the ability to launch a potentially devastating conventional attack in Central Europe with little warning."[42] General Alexander Haig, as supreme allied commander in Europe, suggested that NATO would have at least eight days' warning of an attack. His estimate was said to be based on a detailed study of Warsaw Pact readiness. Reportedly, some analysts felt that Haig's estimate was too high.[43] A third, perhaps prudently conservative estimate of the time needed by the Warsaw Pact to prepare a two-front attack would be four days. Reinforcements would presumably arrive after the onset of hostilities. Alternatively, the Warsaw Pact could engage in lengthier preparations for a larger attack.

A THREE-FRONT ATTACK. Polish and Czechoslovak forces as well as the Soviet Northern Group of Forces (NGF) based in Poland would be added to the Soviet and East German forces to form a three-front attack, which would command thirty-eight divisions' worth of manpower in major combat units. The Polish and Czechoslovak armies would contribute about 40 percent of this combat potential. The time needed to organize a three-front attack could vary, according to General Haig's 1977 comments, anywhere from eight to fifteen days.[44] A prudently

41. Drew Middleton, *New York Times,* September 5, 1980.
42. Senator Sam Nunn and Senator Dewey F. Bartlett, *NATO and the New Soviet Threat,* a report to the Senate Armed Services Committee, 95 Cong. 1 sess. (GPO, 1977), pp. 4–6.
43. Drew Middleton, *New York Times,* September 15, 1977.
44. Ibid.

conservative compromise might settle on eleven days as the length of time needed for preparation.

The extent of Poland's and Czechoslovakia's participation in a war is the bigger question. The Warsaw Treaty of 1955 does not oblige any member to participate in military operations outside the treaty area. It is thought that under any circumstances the reliability of the Czechoslovak Army would be very low, while that of the Polish Army could range from acceptable to very low, depending in part on Polish perceptions of West German behavior.[45] Some NATO analysts believe that these armies would be used merely to conduct minor military operations and to guard and maintain supply lines,[46] which would considerably reduce the Warsaw Pact's combat potential. Of course, if one or more Eastern European countries openly rebelled against Soviet domination (a popular assumption in forecasts of a European war), the situation would be far worse from Moscow's perspective. In such a case, Soviet supply lines would be threatened and substantial Soviet reinforcements might well have to be diverted to restore order. The extent of the Eastern European contribution—particularly the Polish and Czechoslovak—to anything larger than a two-front attack makes the strength of such an offensive open to serious question.

A SIX-FRONT ATTACK. The Baltic, Belorussian, and Carpathian military districts of the Soviet Army presumably would be transformed into operational fronts in a six-front attack. They would add thirty-three divisions, most of them now at category 2 or 3 levels of readiness, to the forces available. A six-front attack would command about fifty-nine divisions' worth of manpower in major combat units, with the expected Polish and Czechoslovak contribution amounting to about 25 percent.

Important differences exist regarding the amount of time thought needed to organize a six-front offensive involving over one million troops. The U.S. Defense Department since the late 1960s has usually assumed that about four weeks of Warsaw Pact mobilization would precede a reinforced attack. But around 1976, evidence of improvements in the Eastern European transportation system led to suggestions that Soviet divisions from western Russia might reach Eastern European assembly areas in half the time—at a rate of three divisions per day,

---

45. Dale R. Herspring and Ivan Volgyes, "Political Reliability in the Eastern European Warsaw Pact Armies," *Armed Forces and Society,* vol. 6 (Winter 1980), pp. 286–91.

46. Drew Middleton, *New York Times,* September 5, 1980.

beginning on the fifth day of mobilization, or even at a rate of four divisions per day.[47] That suggests only fourteen days might be needed to move the thirty-three divisions from the western military districts.

Estimates of division movement rates are relatively uncontroversial. There is, however, a great deal of controversy about the amount of time that would be needed to marshal the necessary transport, mobilize reservists, and raise the combat readiness of the numerous category 2 and 3 divisions.[48] Two CBO analysts feel that those who support the idea of a fourteen-day mobilization period "tend to disregard command and control problems during the movement (the movement of forces . . . would involve division- and corps-size units transferring across each other's lines of supply) and to ignore potential problems in getting units ready to move and into position after the move."[49] William Kaufmann notes that "it seems to take the Red Army about three months to set up a major attack force—whether against Czechoslovakia in 1968, Afghanistan in 1979, or Poland in 1981."[50] These operations were conducted on Soviet terms, however, and one could argue that the Warsaw Pact would feel compelled to hasten its preparations for an attack on NATO. Since the overall readiness and mobilization capabilities of the Warsaw Pact are so uncertain, it seems prudent to consider a six-week preparation period for a six-front attack as well as two-week and four-week periods.

AN AUGMENTED SIX-FRONT ATTACK. There is no telling which military districts would contribute to an augmented six-front attack or how many more forces would be deployed. In light of requirements for Soviet forces elsewhere (see appendix B), it is assumed that the augmentation would include divisions from the Kiev, Moscow, Volga, Ural, and

---

47. Fischer, *Defending the Central Front*, p. 21. See also Wiener and Lewis, *Warsaw Pact Armies*, p. 125.

48. Warsaw Pact logistical systems would depend on mobilization of trucks from the civil sector; it is not known how long that would take. As for the mobilization of reservists, the Soviet system is designed for the efficient rounding out of understrength units. Reportedly, however, the August 1980 mobilization of reservists for a possible move into Poland "was marked by extraordinary confusion, disorder and wholesale desertions." Kevin Klose, *Washington Post*, February 13, 1981.

49. CBO, *Assessing the NATO/Warsaw Pact Military Balance*, p. 23. Skeptics sometimes draw attention to problems encountered in past operations. For example, see Les Aspin, "A Surprise Attack on NATO: Refocusing the Debate," *Congressional Record*, daily ed., February 7, 1977, pp. H911-13. Despite its focus, some of the points contained are relevant to the debate over a reinforced attack.

50. William W. Kaufmann, "The Defense Budget," in Joseph A. Pechman, ed., *Setting National Priorities: The 1982 Budget* (Brookings Institution, 1981), p. 142.

48 *Defense of Central Europe*

Central Asian military districts. Over half the divisions involved would be category 2 or 3 in readiness. The total force might well command about eighty divisions' worth of manpower in major combat units. Polish and Czechoslovak contributions would amount to about 20 percent of the total.

The length of time the Warsaw Pact would need to organize an augmented six-front attack of one hundred and twenty divisions has been estimated at as little as four weeks and as much as three months. The former seems an unrealistically short time in which to mobilize large numbers of low-readiness units and transport them over considerable distances from the Soviet interior.[51] While it appears that the Warsaw Pact could easily take three months to prepare a one-hundred-and-twenty-division attack, sixty days may be a conservative possibility.

NATO Forces

The ground forces most immediately available for defense of NATO's central front are those on active duty in West Germany. Other forces in Western Europe could be mobilized within a week or so, while reinforcements from the United States would arrive over several months (see table 3-3 and appendix C).

ACTIVE FORCES IN WEST GERMANY. At full strength, NATO forces on active duty in West Germany command about twenty-one divisions' worth of manpower in major combat units. Some of these forces are kept at high readiness; they include the U.S. armored cavalry regiments, about one-fifth of West Germany's divisional forces, and, presumably, selected units (reconnaissance battalions, for example) from other allied armies.[52] Other U.S. forces are fully manned but would take at least one day to reach the front.[53] Other allied units tend to be less than fully manned, with shortfalls apparently most common at the support end;[54] they would need about three days to achieve wartime strengths and

---

51. CBO, *U.S. Ground Forces*, p. 21, suggests four weeks. In fairness, this analysis seems to be based on different assumptions—for example, that the Soviet Union would draw on supposedly higher-readiness divisions stationed in regions near NATO's flanks. Defense Department analysts, however, have considered this an unlikely move.

52. Seven of West Germany's twelve division-equivalents (eleven divisions plus three airborne brigades) are stationed in forward areas. One-third of these are kept on four-hour alert. Canby, *Short (And Long) War Responses*, pp. 30, 70.

53. Fischer, *Defending the Central Front*, p. 21.

54. For instance, while their wartime strength is 11,500, British armored divisions

perhaps replace conscript trainees.⁵⁵ In addition, NATO would need some time to set up its command and logistical systems. It is impossible to forecast how far NATO would go in making the transition to a wartime posture before full mobilization. As a practical matter, this study assumes that the highly ready forces would be available on the first day of mobilization and other active forces stationed in West Germany within three days.

OTHER WESTERN EUROPEAN FORCES. Other forces in Western Europe would contribute almost another thirteen divisions' worth of manpower in major combat units. Active units needing only individuals to augment peacetime strengths and replace conscript trainees are expected to be fully manned and ready to move by the third day of mobilization, and reserve battalions and cadred brigades or regiments by the fifth day.⁵⁶ Many of the combat units in West Germany's Territorial Army may actually be capable of more rapid mobilization. The experiences of Israel—another front-line state—demonstrate that it is possible to mobilize reserve brigades within twenty-four hours; and it is reported that 30,000 West German reservists can be called up on just a few hours' notice.⁵⁷ Indeed, a Rand Corporation expert on European territorial forces states that West Germany's home defense forces "are considered capable of being built up to full strength in about two days."⁵⁸ This study assumes, with allowance for travel time, that all of these forces, including three heavy regiments that are wholly unmanned in peacetime, would be available in the first week of mobilization, some within a day or two.⁵⁹

---

normally have 8,500 men. IISS, *Military Balance, 1980–1981*, p. vii. This study assumes that 1,200 men from Britain's 4,000-man field force are temporarily stationed in Northern Ireland at any given time.

55. Fischer, *Defending the Central Front*, p. 17; West German Minister of Defense, *White Paper 1979*, pp. 152–54, 163, 208. The West Germans insist that in-unit training of new conscripts does not prejudice operational readiness.

56. Fischer, *Defending the Central Front*, p. 20.

57. Edward Luttwak and Dan Horowitz, *The Israeli Army* (Harper and Row, 1975), p. 180; Michael Getler, *Washington Post*, March 26, 1977.

58. Horst Mendershausen, *Territorial Defense in NATO and Non-NATO Europe*, R-1184-ISA, prepared for U.S. Department of Defense, Office of the Assistant Secretary of Defense/International Security (Santa Monica, Calif.: Rand Corp., 1973), p. 48.

59. In peacetime, West Germany mans one of its home defense brigades at 85 percent strength, two at 65 percent, and the remaining three at 52 percent. The light home defense regiments are basic infantry units with simple equipment. West German Minister of Defense, *White Paper 1979*, p. 154; information provided by the Washington embassy of the Federal Republic of Germany.

Table 3-3. NATO's Ground Order of Battle for the Central Front

Country	Active forces		Reserve forces
	In West Germany	Stationed elsewhere	
Belgium	1 corps HQ, ⅔ mechanized division	⅔ mechanized division[a]	⅔ mechanized division
Canada	1 mechanized brigade	None[b]	None
Denmark	None	1 mechanized division	None
France	1 corps HQ, 3 armored divisions[c]	2 corps HQ, 5 armored divisions, 4 mechanized divisions[d]	None[e]
Great Britain	1 corps HQ, 4 armored divisions, 1 infantry brigade	2 infantry brigades[f]	Numerous minor units assigned to round out or augment regular units
Netherlands	⅓ mechanized division	1 corps HQ, 1⅔ mechanized divisions	1 mechanized division, 1 infantry brigade
United States	2 corps HQ, 2 armored cavalry regiments, 2 armored divisions, 2 mechanized divisions, 1 armored brigade, 2 mechanized brigades[g]	*With prepositioned equipment:* 1 corps HQ, 1 armored cavalry regiment, 2 armored divisions, 1 mechanized division, 1 mechanized division with 1 of 3 brigades forward-deployed[h]	3 corps HQ, 1 mechanized division, 2 armored divisions, 5 infantry divisions, 1 Marine division, 4 armored cavalry regiments, 4 armored brigades, 2 mechanized brigades assigned

		Without prepositioned equipment: 1 corps HQ, 2 mechanized divisions with 2 active brigades each, 1 infantry division, 2 infantry divisions with 2 active brigades each, 1 airborne division, 1 air-mobile division, 1 armored brigade, 1 infantry brigade[i]	to round out active divisions, 6 separate mechanized brigades, 2 infantry brigades assigned to round out active divisions, 5 separate infantry brigades[j]
West Germany	3 corps HQ, 6 armored divisions, 5 mechanized divisions, 3 airborne brigades[k]	None	6 home defense brigades, 3 heavy home defense regiments, 12 light home defense regiments[l]

Sources: *Department of Defense Annual Report, Fiscal Year 1982*, pp. 132–33; *Annual Defense Department Report, FY1976 and FY1977*, pp. 142–44, 215–16, 218–21; IISS, *Military Balance, 1980–1981*, pp. 6–9, 21–30; West German Minister of Defense, *White Paper 1979: The Security of the Federal Republic of Germany and the Development of the Federal Armed Forces* (Federal Minister of Defense, 1979), pp. 150–56.

a. Assumes that one half of a paracommando regiment would be assigned to NATO's mobile force and the other half withheld for home defense.
b. Other forces appear to be earmarked for NATO's northern flank.
c. Excludes a brigade in West Berlin.
d. Excludes 1 alpine division and forces stationed outside Europe or oriented toward intervention.
e. Assumes reserves would be withheld.
f. Each infantry brigade consists of 3 active and 2 reserve battalions; 1 brigade, earmarked for NATO's strategic reserve, could be sent to its northern or southern flank. Forces stationed outside Europe or apparently earmarked for NATO's northern flank are not included. Excludes brigade in West Berlin.
g. Excludes an infantry brigade in West Berlin.
h. In addition, 1 armored and 1 mechanized division are assigned 4 brigades, 1 of which is forward-deployed.
i. Assumes that 1 Marine division is earmarked for NATO's flanks and 2 for Asia. Excludes forces for South Korea, Alaska, and Panama. Assumes that in the event of simultaneous contingencies in Southwest and Northeast Asia, 1 mechanized division, 1 airborne division, 1 air-mobile division, and 1 corps would not be available for use in Europe.
j. Excludes 1 training brigade and 4 brigades assigned to special defense missions.
k. Includes 1 mountain division counted as a mechanized division.
l. An additional 3 heavy home defense regiments and 3 light home defense regiments are to be formed by the mid-1980s.

Fischer assumes that postmobilization movement would take one day at most for units based in West Germany and two days for those stationed in Belgium or the Netherlands; that mechanized forces from France would arrive between the third and seventh days of mobilization; and that one brigade from Britain could arrive on the fifth day and another on the ninth day.[60]

PROSPECTIVE U.S. REINFORCEMENTS. Reinforcements from the United States fall into three groups. Forces whose equipment has been prepositioned in West Germany would contribute almost four divisions' worth of manpower in major combat units. Other active forces, when the reserve units that are to round out their strength are included, would contribute seven divisions' worth of manpower in major combat units; this excludes forces presumed earmarked for NATO's flanks, for a three-division Asian contingency, or for special missions.[61] Reserve component forces, excluding those used to round out active units, would contribute another thirteen divisions' worth of men in major combat units.

The arrival times of U.S. ground reinforcements in Europe are uncertain. The U.S. Defense Department assumes that forces with prepositioned equipment would deploy on the central front between six and ten days after mobilization begins.[62] Other U.S.-based units whose equipment must move with them could begin arriving in two weeks. The United States could airlift follow-on reinforcements containing two divisions' worth of men in major combat units within fourteen to thirty

---

60. *Defending the Central Front*, pp. 21, 23. Fischer implies that his British estimate may be overly optimistic and indicates that it assumes quick call-up, deployment without refresher training, and no transportation or reception constraints. His estimate appears reasonable in light of a 1980 exercise in which Britain managed to deploy 30,000 troops in less than a week. Mike Gains, "NATO's Crusader 80," *Flight International*, vol. 118 (October 25, 1980), p. 1569; Drew Middleton, *New York Times*, October 11, 1980.

61. If simultaneous contingencies arose in Southwest and Northeast Asia, however, forces with manpower equivalent to about three divisions (one corps, with one airborne, one air-mobile, and one mechanized division) would presumably be dropped from the list of forces available for Europe.

62. It was the Carter administration's intention to preposition enough equipment by fiscal 1986 so that six divisions could deploy to Europe within ten days of a decision to reinforce. *Department of Defense Annual Report, Fiscal Year 1982*, p. 197. A unit with prepositioned equipment would, however, need one to two days to prepare for deployment, about a day to travel, and four to five days to draw its equipment and reach assembly areas. CBO, *U.S. Airlift Forces: Enhancement Alternatives for NATO and Non-NATO Contingencies*, prepared by John J. Hamre (GPO, 1979), pp. 49–50, 80.

days of mobilization.[63] Around the thirtieth day, forces would presumably begin arriving by sea.[64] Secretary Brown claimed that the United States "should have about as much military dry-cargo shipping as we can use" to move reinforcements to Europe. One constraint on reinforcement would be the readiness of U.S.-based ground units.[65] The additional forces that the Army seems to foresee being deployed by the ninetieth day include eight divisions and fifteen brigades or regiments.[66] This suggests that three of the divisions and almost all the separate brigades or regiments would come from the reserve components, while four of the other five divisions would have to be rounded out by a reserve brigade. This study assumes that, using sealift and airlift, the United States could deploy another eleven divisions' worth of men in major combat units to central Europe between thirty and ninety days after mobilization begins.[67] Obviously, a number of things could disrupt these deployments, including shipping losses to hostile naval action or damage to ports and airfields in Western Europe. And if the United States had to respond to one or more simultaneous contingencies outside Europe, the assets it could devote to moving NATO reinforcements would be significantly reduced.[68]

NATO'S OVERALL GROUND POSTURE. Given the assumptions about NATO's order of battle and its mobilization and deployment rates, the ground combat potential of NATO forces on the central front from mobilization day forward is estimated in table 3-4 in terms of manpower

63. Included are one corps, one airborne division, one air-mobile division, and one armored brigade from the active Army. Author's estimates assume full use of the Civil Reserve Air Fleet and are based on CBO, *U.S. Airlift Forces*, pp. 23, 25, 49, 55.

64. *Department of Defense Annual Report, Fiscal Year 1981*, p. 208. See also Fischer, *Defending the Central Front*, p. 22. Although a sea crossing could take as little as one week, it appears that no forces would arrive by sea before the twenty-fifth day because of the additional time needed to move units to embarkation ports, to marshal the requisite shipping, and—if hostilities were imminent or under way—to counter Soviet naval forces.

65. *Department of Defense Annual Report, Fiscal Year 1981*, p. 208.

66. *Department of Defense Appropriations for 1980*, Hearings before a subcommittee of the House Appropriations Committee, 96 Cong. 1 sess. (GPO, 1979), pt. 2, pp. 682–83.

67. Included are two mechanized and three infantry divisions (with all except for one infantry division requiring a round-out brigade), and one infantry brigade from the active Army; and three corps, one mechanized and two armored divisions, four armored brigades, six mechanized brigades, and four armored cavalry regiments from the reserve components.

68. *Department of Defense Annual Report, Fiscal Year 1982*, p. 197. See also Kaufmann, "The Defense Budget," p. 161–62.

Table 3-4. Number of Men in Major Combat Units Available to NATO, at Selected Times after Mobilization Begins

Country	M-day	M+3	M+5	M+7	M+10	M+14	M+21	M+28	M+35	M+42	M+60	M+75	M+90
						Thousands of men							
Belgium[a]	1	12	23	35	35	35	35	35	35	35	35	35	35
Canada	...	3	3	3	3	3	3	3	3	3	3	3	3
Denmark	...	...	18	18	18	18	18	18	18	18	18	18	18
France[b]	...	49	77	84	84	84	84	84	84	84	84	84	84
Great Britain[c]	3	50	54	54	58	58	58	58	58	58	58	58	58
Netherlands[a]	1	6	35	57	57	57	57	57	57	57	57	57	57
United States[d]	6	95	95	130	182	190	204	218	238	260	317	365	412
West Germany[e]	39	255	255	264	264	264	264	264	264	264	264	264	264
Total manpower	50	470	560	645	701	709	723	737	757	779	836	884	931
						Manpower division equivalents							
Total division equivalents	3	26	31	35	38	39	40	40	41	43	46	48	51

Source: Appendix A.
a. Assumes 1 reconnaissance battalion alert and available on M-day, all forward-deployed forces available by M+3, all active forces deployed by M+5, and all reserve brigades available by M+7.
b. Assumes that 7 divisions are available by M+3, another 4 by M+5, and 1 more by M+7.
c. Assumes that the peacetime field force is alert and available on M-day, all forward-deployed forces are fully manned and deployed by M+3, and 2 additional field forces arrive by M+5 and M+9.
d. Assumes that 2 armored cavalry regiments are available on M-day, all forward-based forces are deployed by M+2, units with prepositioned equipment arrive and deploy between M+6 and M+10, another 2 divisions and 1 brigade deploy between M+11 and M+30, and another 8 divisions and 15 brigades or regiments deploy between M+30 and M+90 at the rate of about 1 division equivalent every 5 days.
e. Assumes that 1/5 of all divisional forces is available on M-day, that all active forces are filled out and deployed and that 6 home defense brigades and 12 light regiments are available by M+3, and that 3 heavy regiments deploy by M+7.

in major combat units. Implicit in the estimates is the assumption that the NATO forces listed would have actually deployed by the times specified.

The Numerical Balance of Forces

The quantitative balance of ground forces in central Europe would depend on the amount of time the Warsaw Pact spends preparing an attack, on NATO's buildup rates, and on the speed with which NATO responds to Warsaw Pact preparations. Although U.S. officials maintain that the West would become aware of Eastern mobilization "in a matter of hours,"[69] it is generally assumed that NATO's mobilization would lag somewhat behind that of its adversary. For planning purposes, Defense Department analysts have usually assumed a lag of seven days.[70] This is the worst delay considered in the following analysis of alternatives to NATO's current posture. Some observers worry that even a seven-day lag might be an optimistic assumption.[71] Of course, NATO might well respond more promptly to warning, a possibility that is allowed for in the analysis.

Different measures are appropriate for assessing the expected effectiveness of a ground force during the various phases of a ground campaign. Force-to-space ratios would probably be most important at the onset, when the defense is just trying to cover the front along defensible frontages. Operational reserves would then be needed to parry attempts by the offense to break through the front line. Eventually,

69. *Annual Defense Department Report, FY 1977*, p. 118.
70. CBO, *Assessing the NATO/Warsaw Pact Military Balance*, pp. 21–22.
71. One analyst notes, for instance, that NATO would need time to digest intelligence reports and convene the North Atlantic Council; that the council would need to reach unanimous agreement before NATO could declare the higher alert levels necessary for reserve mobilization and large-scale troop movements; that Western decisionmakers might be plagued throughout by disbelief about the imminency of war; and that they might also be reluctant to risk provocation by sending armored forces to the border, especially if Moscow appeared paranoid and justified its military preparations on defensive grounds. Betts, *Surprise Attack*, pp. 170–77. But the length of NATO's lag is impossible to predict. The most that can be said is that NATO's defensive prospects are inextricably linked to a prompt political decision to deploy NATO forces to the frontier to defend against a short-warning attack. If NATO fails to respond to warning in a timely manner, it could be defeated by the relatively small force that Moscow might manage to assemble in a few days.

as losses and enemy penetrations strain the defense, force ratios would become most important.

Assumptions as to what is needed in terms of force densities, operational reserves, and force ratios, as to how quickly the Warsaw Pact could prepare an attack, and as to how quickly NATO would mobilize in response to warning are combined to construct the curves in figure 3-2, comparing NATO's current posture against three alternatives.

A HIGH-STANDARDS NATO POSTURE. The most stringent of the three alternative postures supposes that NATO would be capable of deploying the equivalent of thirty divisions on the first day of mobilization. This density of twenty-five kilometers per division represents what is considered normal frontage, while the high peacetime readiness constitutes a hedge against short warning, delayed NATO response, or both. By the seventh day, NATO would also have a capacity for deploying the equivalent of sixty divisions. This responds to the possibilities that Moscow could launch a reinforced (six-front) attack after two weeks' preparation and that NATO mobilization might lag by one week, as well as to the argument that—even with normal coverage of the front—50 percent of the defense force should be withheld as operational reserves. By the twenty-third day, NATO would be able to deploy the equivalent of sixty-seven divisions. Again allowing for a seven-day lag in its mobilization, this would enable NATO to maintain a 1.2:1 force ratio against an attack by the equivalent of eighty divisions launched after only thirty days of preparation.

A LOW-STANDARDS NATO POSTURE. The least demanding of the three alternatives assumes that NATO would be capable of deploying the equivalent of thirteen divisions by the sixth day of mobilization. This density of almost sixty kilometers per division represents the thinnest of minimums, while the mobilization target implies that the Warsaw Pact would need at least eight days to prepare an attack and that the start of NATO mobilization would lag by no more than two days. Presumably, NATO would eventually want to achieve normal coverage of the front and provide some operational reserves—but when and how many? This alternative also envisions a capacity for deploying the equivalent of forty divisions by the fortieth day, which would enable a promptly mobilizing NATO to withhold 25 percent of its forces as operational reserves to meet a six-front attack assumed to require six weeks of preparation. By the eighty-eighth day NATO would be able to deploy the equivalent of forty-four divisions. Again assuming a two-day mobilization lag, this

Figure 3-2. Pattern of Mobilization of NATO Forces and Proposed Alternatives

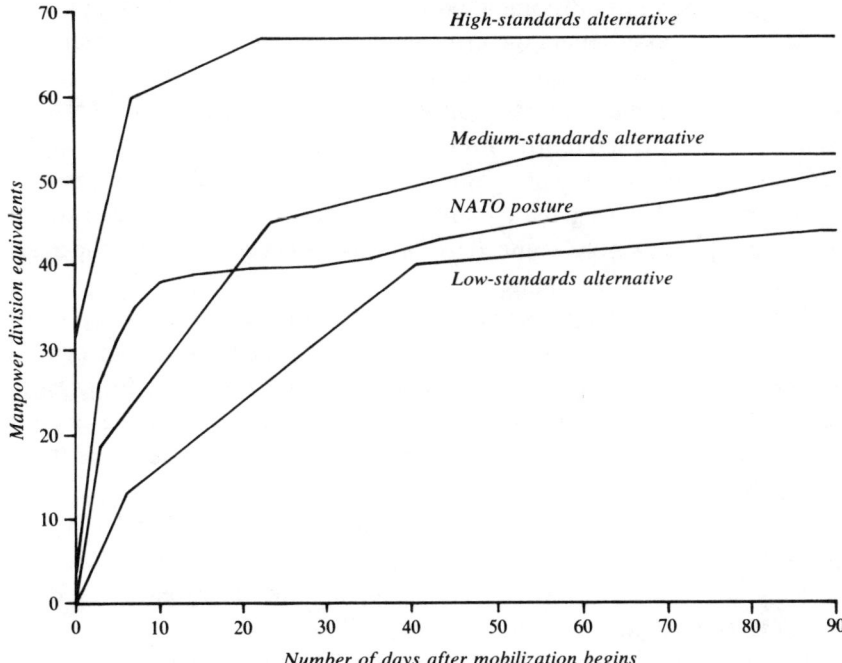

would allow NATO to maintain a force ratio of about 1.8:1 against a force equivalent to eighty divisions that needed ninety days to prepare an attack.

A MEDIUM-STANDARDS POSTURE. As a compromise between the high and low standards, NATO is assumed to be capable of deploying the equivalent of nineteen divisions by the third day of mobilization. Thus, NATO could achieve initial densities of forty kilometers per division and maintain a hedge against either short warning or delayed response. By the twenty-third day NATO would also have a capacity for deploying forty-five divisions. This would permit NATO to maintain normal coverage of the front while withholding one-third of its forces as operational reserves, all in time to meet—after a five-day mobilization lag—a six-front attack that required four weeks' preparation. And by the fifty-fifth day NATO would be able to deploy the equivalent of fifty-three divisions, which would enable it to maintain a force ratio of about 1.5:1 against an augmented six-front attack that needed about sixty days to organize itself.

NATO'S CURRENT POSTURE. The Western nations' capability for building up their ground combat potential, depicted as the NATO pattern in figure 3-2, never meets the criteria identified as the most-demanding alternative. Western buildup capabilities would exceed those represented as the middle alternative during the first two weeks or so of NATO mobilization. Subsequently, however, the West would lag behind the ground combat potential prescribed for this medium-standards posture. At all times, NATO's ground combat potential would be superior to the minimal requirements advanced by various observers that form the basis for the low-standards posture.

None of these comparisons permits any firm conclusions regarding the adequacy of the quantitative balance of ground forces in central Europe. More defending forces would provide the basis for greater confidence in peacetime but would not guarantee wartime victory for NATO. Actual combat would involve too many uncertainties. And there remain major uncertainties about the shape of the curves in figure 3-2. Would Eastern European forces actually join a Soviet attack? Would NATO respond to warning in a timely manner? Would some unforeseen contingency draw away U.S. reinforcements previously earmarked for NATO? The list could go on.

On balance, it appears that the numerical ground balance in central Europe cannot afford NATO high confidence, but neither should it leave the West unduly pessimistic about its defensive prospects. To the extent that NATO would experience shortfalls in ground combat potential, figure 3-2 indicates that NATO's problems would come several weeks into mobilization. It appears that NATO may well have scrimped on longer-term capabilities to meet a perceived short-warning threat.

Other Factors

Since the numerical balance of ground forces could easily be inconclusive, other factors might have a decisive impact on the outcome of a conflict. The availability of prepared defensive positions; the readiness of active and reserve forces; logistics; command, control, and communications; and air power are all areas in which strengths and weaknesses could make a great difference in the outcome of a conflict.

PREPARED DEFENSIVE POSITIONS. According to many soldiers and historians, prepared defensive positions can slow an attacker's advance.

Since none now exist along the central front, defensive positions presumably would be created only after NATO forces deploy to their wartime locations. To provide a prepared defense over a depth of thirty kilometers would take about twenty days and to fortify this zone would take about forty days, one historian suggests; the former would double and the latter quadruple the time otherwise needed by an attacker to advance that distance.[72] Thus if warning of an attack was not too short and was promptly acted on, NATO could set up prepared or fortified defenses that, presumably, would somewhat offset the Warsaw Pact's quantitative edge in a six-front or an augmented six-front attack.

READINESS. A unit's performance in combat depends in large measure on its combat readiness. Reserve units, an appreciable number of which are included in Warsaw Pact and NATO mobilization plans, tend to be less ready than their active counterparts. According to Fischer, their readiness is related to their size; he assumes that battalions normally can be kept at full readiness, and that brigades that maintain at least a skeleton headquarters and command structure can also be kept combat-ready.[73] Secretary Schlesinger maintained that U.S. experience indicated that reserve brigades can be made ready for deployment much sooner than reserve divisions, which would apparently require up to fourteen weeks of uninterrupted training to become combat-ready.[74] Most Western European reserve units are brigade-sized or smaller and their state of readiness would not create significant problems.[75] Nor are the separate brigades or regiments from the U.S. reserve components that would be deployed during the early weeks of mobilization likely to suffer from serious deficiencies in readiness.[76] However, the National Guard divisions that supposedly would be deployed sixty to ninety days into mobilization are unlikely to be ready for combat by the designated

---

72. Colonel T. N. Dupuy, *Numbers, Predictions, and War: Using History to Evaluate Combat Factors and Predict the Outcome of Battles* (Bobbs-Merrill, 1979), p. 211.

73. *Defending the Central Front*, p. 20.

74. *Annual Defense Department Report, FY 1975*, pp. 99–100. See also Martin Binkin, *U.S. Reserve Forces: The Problem of the Weekend Warrior* (Brookings Institution, 1974), pp. 10–11.

75. Fischer, *Defending the Central Front*, p. 20.

76. Any personnel or equipment shortfalls, which are overlooked here, could impede readiness. It appears that the reserve brigades assigned to round out active divisions maintain high readiness. See *Department of Defense Authorization for Appropriations for Fiscal Year 1981*, Hearings before the Senate Armed Services Committee, 96 Cong. 2 sess. (GPO, 1980), pt. 2, pp. 706–07.

time of their deployment. It is impossible to say how much this might degrade NATO's capabilities.

The readiness, and thus the military effectiveness, of many of the Warsaw Pact's category 2 and 3 divisions is the source of greatest uncertainty.[77] They would constitute over 20 percent of the divisions deployed for a three-front attack, 45 percent of those involved in a six-front attack, and almost 60 percent of those participating in an augmented six-front attack. To achieve full readiness, category 2 divisions would need twenty-five to thirty days and category 3 would require fifty to one hundred and twenty days.[78] Perhaps the most that can reasonably be said about lower readiness among them is that it would somewhat degrade the actual combat capability of the Warsaw Pact. The shorter the preparation time for an attack—particularly one reinforced from Russia—the more troublesome the deficiency could be. It could well offset the force ratio benefits that the Warsaw Pact might seek through shorter preparation times.

LOGISTICAL SUPPORT. A major weakness of Warsaw Pact armies is their level of logistical support. They have traditionally been willing to trade off support assets for more immediate combat power. (They have also emphasized unit rather than individual replacement of combat losses, which produces additional marginal savings in manpower.)[79] Indeed, the force structure of the Warsaw Pact appears to Fischer and other analysts to be focused on using extra combat power "to win a war before its own logistic and maintenance deficiencies overwhelm it."[80] Canby argues that Warsaw Pact operations would be designed to succeed despite sparse support; he believes that relatively scarce logistical assets would be concentrated on a few narrow sectors, where they are really needed, "to provide a support framework in which combat divisions and even armies can be used like drill tips on a high-speed drill—to be ground down and replaced until penetration occurs."[81] However, during

---

77. *Department of Defense Annual Report, Fiscal Year 1982*, p. 74.

78. Fischer, *Defending the Central Front*, pp. 20–21, 23. See also Wiener and Lewis, *Warsaw Pact Armies*, pp. 59–60; *Allocation of Resources*, Hearings, pt. 4, p. 250; Record, *Sizing Up the Soviet Army*, pp. 21–22; Michael Getler, *Washington Post*, June 7, 1973.

79. Lawrence and Record, *U.S. Force Structure*, p. 79. They advocate adoption of a unit replacement system by the U.S. Army.

80. Fischer, *Defending the Central Front*, p. 14.

81. "After penetration the divisions rapidly exploiting their advantage no longer require extensive support." Canby, *Military Doctrine and Technology*, pp. 10–11.

the unopposed invasion of Czechoslovakia in 1968, one account maintains, a breakdown of transportation and supply services threatened to paralyze Soviet forces during the first week of the operation, and they would have lacked many essential items after the first twenty-four hours of combat.[82] But improvements have been made since 1968. The chairman of the Joint Chiefs of Staff reports that the Warsaw Pact's stocks of goods to be used in the initial stages of combat are adequate, though the International Institute for Strategic Studies suggests that the Eastern European countries may well be short of supplies for sustained combat.[83] Transportation is apparently far more effective now than in the past and maintenance has improved. Logistical requirements, however, have presumably increased also as Warsaw Pact divisions have been assigned additional artillery and other weapons.[84] And American officials claim that the Warsaw Pact's "maintenance system has long been a problem and may prove inadequate in full-scale operations," lending credence to Fischer's suggestion that mechanical breakdowns in their armor "might begin to rival battle casualties" after a week or two of combat.[85] Thus, the ability of Warsaw Pact armies to fight effectively for very long remains open to serious question on several grounds.

There would probably be logistical problems for NATO too; U.S. stocks of goods used in combat are expected to "satisfy most requirements at the outset," but some of the other NATO nations have supplies "for only a relatively short period of intensive combat." Moreover, "lack of standardization and limited means of transportation" would hamper emergency redistribution of goods among national forces.[86] It also appears that the U.S. Army would experience serious shortages of trained personnel for several months after the start of mobilization.[87]

---

82. Leo Heiman, "Soviet Invasion Weaknesses," *Military Review*, vol. 49 (August 1969), pp. 42, 43, quoted in Record, *Sizing Up the Soviet Army*, pp. 45–46. See also Wiener and Lewis, *Warsaw Pact Armies*, p. 67.

83. *United States Military Posture for FY 1981*, pp. 19–20; IISS, *Military Balance, 1980–81*, p. 113.

84. See U.S. Department of the Army, *Handbook on Soviet Ground Forces*, FM 30-40 (GPO, 1976), app. A; IISS, *Military Balance, 1978–1979*, pp. 102–03.

85. *United States Military Posture for FY 1981*, p. 75; Fischer, *Defending the Central Front*, p. 14.

86. *United States Military Posture for FY 1981*, p. 20

87. The U.S. Army structure calls for 1.73 million soldiers upon full mobilization. Because of shortages in reserve component units and low levels of individual reservists, however, it appears that the Army would have only 1.46 million men—84 percent of its requirement—on hand ninety days after mobilization begins. It is feared that forward-

And until French territory becomes available, many of NATO's supply lines, running from north to south in forward areas, could easily be interdicted. The IISS concludes that "the former NATO superiority in forward-area logistics has probably now gone, though there is some inherent advantage in operating on home territory."[88]

COMMAND, CONTROL, AND COMMUNICATIONS. Warsaw Pact armies, according to U.S. Defense Department officials, enjoy significant advantages in command, control, and communications (C3), but they also depend on C3 more than NATO forces do. The Warsaw Pact's communications systems are "redundant, well-protected and highly interoperable," while NATO's do not yet have these qualities.[89] The advantages the Warsaw Pact enjoys, however, reflect a traditional Soviet emphasis on tight control from the top. Secretary Brown maintained that "the inflexibility inherent in such a system, coupled with the tendency of seniors to distrust their subordinates and to provide them with only minimum essential information on the evolving tactical situation," could hurt Warsaw Pact operations in a "rapidly changing, often unpredictable battlefield situation, particularly if their means of control are disrupted."[90] While the Soviet Army has long emphasized radio-electronic combat, the U.S. Army has recently deployed electronic warfare battalions in West Germany to improve its capacity for disrupting enemy communications. For the time being, one may suppose that any conflict would pit the East's superior C3 systems and rigid style against the West's inferior systems and superior initiative.

AIR POWER. The West has traditionally counted on air power. While the situation has become more uncertain in recent years, the West probably retains some edge. General Jones has maintained that the balance of tactical aircraft is much closer than the ground balance. Although the Warsaw Pact stations more aircraft in central Europe, "the

---

deployed and early deploying units would have to fight at less than wartime strengths, that later deploying units and the U.S. base structure would have to be stripped of trained personnel to replace casualties and fill early deploying units, and that severe shortages of critical combat and medical skills would arise. Although various initiatives have reduced its size in recent years, officials are unsure whether these can wholly eliminate the potential initial shortfall in trained manpower. Maj. Gen. William R. Berkman, USA, "Reserves: Expanded Missions, Limited Resources," *Army*, vol. 30 (October 1980), pp. 166–69; *Department of Defense Annual Report, Fiscal Year 1982*, p. 288; information provided by the Department of the Army.

 88. IISS, *Military Balance, 1980–1981*, p. 113.
 89. *United States Military Posture for FY 1982*, pp. 37–38.
 90. *Department of Defense Annual Report, Fiscal Year 1982*, pp. 74–75.

balance would become more nearly even after reinforcement, especially as aircraft arrive from the United States."[91] His statement reflects, in part, an appreciation of qualitative differences. The West "has a higher proportion of multi-purpose aircraft" that offer better performance overall, "especially in range, payload and all-weather capability."[92] This stems from the traditional emphasis of NATO air forces on air superiority and support of ground troops through interdiction or close air support. The Warsaw Pact, on the other hand, has traditionally assigned its air force to defense of its home air space and has left its ground forces to provide for their own fire support and air defense. During the 1970s, however, new generations of aircraft improved the Soviet air arm's ability to undertake independent air operations against NATO's nuclear weapon sites, airfields, command centers, and equipment stocks, and to thereby lend indirect support to Warsaw Pact ground forces.[93]

The ability of NATO's air forces to provide effective ground support would depend in large part on their ability to survive the air attacks and ground-based air defenses of the Warsaw Pact. Because NATO has fewer airfields and aircraft shelters than its adversary, it would presumably be at some disadvantage in meeting the first threat. But NATO has been deploying new fighters, such as the F-15 and F-16, and airborne warning and control systems (AWACS) are expected to give NATO "a considerable advantage in battle management."[94] The 1973 Middle East war demonstrated that ground-based air defenses can be devastating.[95] Since then, however, Western air forces have developed new electronic countermeasures and tactics to meet the threat.[96] Although the need to suppress opposing air defenses would divert some resources, the striking power of its tactical air forces is still considered one of NATO's

---

91. *United States Military Posture for FY 1981*, p. 19.

92. IISS, *Military Balance, 1980–1981*, p. 113. Another source indicates that NATO's air forces can drop three times more tonnage than the Warsaw Pact's can at a range of 100 miles, and seven times more at a range of 200 miles. Blaker and Hamilton, *Assessing the NATO/Warsaw Pact Military Balance*, p. 37.

93. See William D. White, *U.S. Tactical Air Power: Missions, Forces, and Costs* (Brookings Institution, 1974), pp. 61–73; Robert P. Berman, *Soviet Air Power in Transition* (Brookings Institution, 1978), pp. 66–73.

94. *United States Military Posture for FY 1981*, p. 19.

95. For one account, see Roy M. Braybrook, "Is It Goodbye to Ground Attack?" *Air International*, vol. 10 (May 1976), p. 245.

96. Such efforts seem to have paid off in the 1982 Israeli campaign against Syrian air defenses in Lebanon.

strengths.[97] An ability by Western air forces to provide effective ground support at critical times and places—against a standing-start attack or impending breakthrough, for instance—would help offset any numerical superiority that Warsaw Pact armies might have.

Thus in the many conceivable cases where the numerical balance of ground forces would not clearly favor either side, other factors could have a decisive impact on the outcome of a conflict. One implication of the findings here is that there is probably not much room for overall reductions in NATO's active and reserve force levels. Indeed, it could be argued that modest additions to the NATO force structure are in order. In particular, allowances—in the form of more and better reserve forces, for instance—might prudently be made for the possibility of unexpected demands on U.S. forces from one or more contingencies outside Europe. But if this does not seem a serious threat, NATO should focus on making improvements in areas other than force structure, since analysis of the numerical balance does not point to major force structure deficiencies. The West might well work to exploit the advantages it has in such matters as command and control, logistics, and air power.

97. IISS, *Military Balance, 1980–1981*, pp. 110, 113–14.

CHAPTER FOUR

SHOULD THE U.S. CONTRIBUTION TO NATO CHANGE?

MANY disparate proposals for changing the NATO side of the conventional military equation in central Europe have been advanced in recent years. This is hardly surprising, if for no other reason than that the equation there is so difficult to define. Varying interpretations of the military situation coupled with diverse strategic and political viewpoints have inspired suggestions for increasing, decreasing, or redirecting the U.S. ground force contribution for central Europe. There is fairly widespread agreement, at least among American observers, that the Western European allies should somehow increase their efforts. Several schemes have been put forth for integrating changes in the U.S. and allied ground contributions.

Increasing the U.S. Contribution

Soviet gains in nuclear weaponry have raised unacceptable doubts, for many observers, about the credibility of America's nuclear guarantee and NATO's strategy of flexible response. Such concerns have existed since at least the early 1960s, when Moscow first acquired an ability to strike the American homeland with nuclear weapons; they have been aggravated by the Soviet Union's attainment of nuclear parity with the United States. "Soviet essential equivalence in the nuclear balance," Senator Nunn maintains, "must be met by NATO essential equivalence in the conventional balance."[1] Modernization of NATO's long-range theater nuclear weapons, which some Western European leaders strongly

---

1. Sam Nunn, "Defense Budget and Defense Capabilities," in W. Scott Thompson, ed., *National Security in the 1980s: From Weakness to Strength* (San Francisco: Institute for Contemporary Studies, 1980), p. 388.

support as one way of achieving a more equal East-West balance in those forces, may also require a raising of the nuclear threshold. But the directors of the Atlantic community's four most prestigious foreign affairs councils warn that "a renewed malaise about the use of nuclear weapons in Europe is likely to characterize the domestic politics of various European countries and could result in opposition to the deployment of nuclear weapons."[2] In any case, past administrations have maintained that the United States must set an example before expecting its allies to increase their efforts, even in the defense of their own territory.

Additional Active Forces

Secretary of Defense Caspar Weinberger suggested at one point that the Army should add two divisions to its active force structure, which with nondivisional support units included would increase the Army's strength by about 80,000 men. Options considered have included filling out understrength divisions, creating one or two divisions from scratch, using independent brigades as the core of new divisions, or combining some of these measures.[3] Two analysts in the Congressional Budget Office have pointed to a need for the equivalent of two to five more armored divisions, to help NATO meet the threat of a one-hundred-twenty-division attack. While leaving open the possibility of achieving some of this increase through weapons modernization, they foresaw the addition of as many as 115,000 men.[4] Weinberger's proposal would raise the Army's active-duty strength by 10 percent, while the one from the CBO could involve as much as a 15 percent increase.

Such proposals face the possible constraints of limited U.S. abilities to attract recruits and to move forces overseas. The Army had only uneven success during the late 1970s in enlisting enough qualified people

---

2. Karl Kaiser, director, Forschungsinstitut der Deutschen Gesellschaft für Auswärtige Politik (Bonn); Winston Lord, president, Council on Foreign Relations (New York); Thierry de Montbrial, director, Institut Français des Relations Internationales (Paris); David Watt, director, Royal Institute of International Affairs (London), *Western Security: What Has Changed? What Should Be Done?* (New York: Council on Foreign Relations, 1981), p. 26.

3. Richard Halloran, *New York Times,* April 26, 1981.

4. Congressional Budget Office (CBO), *U.S. Ground Forces: Design and Cost Alternatives for NATO and Non-NATO Contingencies,* prepared by Pat Hillier and Nora Slatkin (CBO, 1980), pp. 79–81.

to man the current force structure. Although a number of extra financial incentives have since been offered that appear to have aided recruiting and retention, expansions of the magnitudes suggested would add a billion dollars or more to annual personnel costs. The CBO notes that the manpower costs of a larger force might exceed its own projections and could prompt Congress to consider a return to one form or another of compulsory service.[5] Although some members of Congress and other observers already favor this course, the reinstitution of conscription would be a politically controversial step, one that the Reagan administration has indicated it wants to avoid.

Recruitment constraints aside, most analysts would probably agree with the view of Eisenhower's defense secretary that there is little use in having more men on active duty than could be transported overseas during the time it takes to mobilize the reserves.[6] William Kaufmann argues by a similar standard that "at present, the United States has too large a force structure" because it does not have the capacity "to move many of the more or less ready ground units in what is considered to be a timely fashion."[7] Improvements now programmed will not substantially increase movement rates until at least the mid-1980s. As chapter 3 suggests, however, the three National Guard divisions apparently earmarked for deployment to central Europe during the first ninety days of mobilization might be unable to achieve full readiness within that time. Substituting additional active divisions for them would presumably eliminate this problem. However, the overall costs from 1982 to 1989 of expanding the active force structure would amount to an estimated $18 billion for two fully supported armored divisions, or about $45 billion for five.[8] A less costly alternative, favored by Kaufmann and others, would be to raise the readiness of reserve component forces.

The addition of active forces could lessen or eliminate the probable shortfall in force structure predicted if two or more other contingencies

---

5. For estimates of the cost of procuring additional manpower, see Richard Halloran, *New York Times*, April 26, 1981; CBO, *Resources for Defense: A Review of Key Issues for Fiscal Years 1982–1986*, prepared by Dov S. Zakheim (U.S. Government Printing Office, 1981), pp. 91–92.

6. Cited in Glenn H. Snyder, "The 'New Look' of 1953," in Warner R. Schilling, Paul Y. Hammond, and Glenn H. Snyder, *Strategy, Politics, and Defense Budgets* (Columbia University Press, 1962), p. 461.

7. William W. Kaufmann, "The Defense Budget," in Joseph A. Pechman, ed., *Setting National Priorities: The 1982 Budget* (Brookings Institution, 1981), p. 172.

8. Estimates based on CBO, *U.S. Ground Forces*, pp. 84, 86–87.

coincide with one in Europe. Again, Kaufmann argues that improvements in reserve readiness would be a less costly way of meeting this possibility. As for the possibility of a one-hundred-twenty-division attack in Europe, observers in the Defense Department tend to regard it as less likely than the CBO analysts do. In any case, it appears that additional forces could not be deployed in time to meet an attacking force of that size, even if the Warsaw Pact needed the longest preparation time that has been suggested. If there were only short warning of an attack, the creation of additional active forces in the United States would, by itself, do nothing to meet the threat.

Additional Prepositioning

The possibility of a six-front attack after just two weeks' preparation and the constraints inherent in existing airlift and sealift assets led the Carter administration to espouse additional prepositioning as the means for speeding American reinforcement of Europe. When it entered office, equipment was prepositioned for only two divisions, as well as one armored cavalry regiment, based in the United States. In 1978 the Carter administration announced a plan to preposition in Europe enough equipment for six divisions based in the United States that could, it hoped, be deployed within ten days. And Zbigniew Brzezinski later revealed a plan to preposition equipment for nine divisions and a number of supporting units, which in theory would be able to deploy in fourteen days.[9] By the end of 1981, equipment had been prepositioned for five divisions, an armored cavalry regiment, and other corps-level support units based in the United States. Assuming a very prompt response to warning and arrival of U.S. units as planned, the prepositioning of equipment for one to four additional divisions would improve NATO's prospects against a six-front attack, even one launched after just two weeks' preparation.

The monetary cost of additional prepositioning is not a significant issue. No equipment is procured specifically for NATO prepositioning. In theory, the prepositioned equipment is borrowed from war reserve stocks and would be replaced by the equipment that a unit deployed to Europe leaves behind in the United States. The costs of maintaining the prepositioned equipment are low, while those for constructing the

9. Estimates based on CBO, *U.S. Airlift Forces: Enhancement Alternatives for NATO and Non-NATO Contingencies,* prepared by John J. Hamre (GPO, 1979), pp. 49, 50, 80.

storage sites are recouped from the NATO infrastructure program. And existing airlift assets appear to be adequate to move the troops within the times projected.[10] The major problems revolve around the overall availability of equipment, the practicability of such rapid reinforcement, and the vulnerability of storage sites.

EQUIPMENT AVAILABILITY. Because war reserve stocks have been too low to fill the requirements of the prepositioning programs initiated by the Carter administration, active and reserve units based in the United States have been forced to give up some of their equipment. The Army has attempted to maintain equipment levels of at least 70 percent for units earmarked for rapid reinforcement and 50 percent for late-deploying reserve units in order to preserve "some reasonable degree of readiness."[11] Both civil and military leaders of the Army indicate that the drawdowns have affected training and reduced the flexibility of the United States to deploy home-based units outside central Europe.[12] Secretary Harold Brown noted that this has been a source of considerable concern and that some shortages will persist for several years, despite increases in Army procurement. He also suggested that equipment shortfalls among active U.S.-based units could delay modernization of the reserve components.[13] Further prepositioning would presumably aggravate these problems. For his part, the Army's chief of staff maintains that "we are approaching the upper limits of feasibility" in the program to preposition materiel in Europe.[14]

PRACTICABILITY. Reinforcement through airlift of forces and prepositioning of materiel is a "relatively untested and difficult process,"[15] Kaufmann warns. And Army officers express skepticism, noting that while the personnel the United States annually flies to West Germany for maneuvers draw their equipment in admittedly short order, the units involved never amount to more than one division. Moreover, most units receive abundant warning of their participation in any of these Reforger exercises.[16] Planning apparently allows for four or five days after arrival

10. Ibid., pp. 47–51.
11. CBO, *Costs of Prepositioning Additional Army Divisions in Europe*, prepared by Nora R. Slatkin (GPO, 1980), p. 5.
12. *The Posture of the Army and Department of the Army Budget Estimates for Fiscal Year 1982*, p. 15.
13. *Department of Defense Annual Report, Fiscal Year 1982*, p. 204.
14. Gen. Edward C. Meyer, USA, *White Paper 1980: A Framework for Molding the Army of the 1980s into a Disciplined, Well-Trained Fighting Force* (GPO, 1980), p. 2.
15. "The Defense Budget," p. 173.
16. Interviews.

for divisions to draw their equipment and deploy to wartime positions. Steven Canby and Kenneth Hunt, however, have warned that unexpected bottlenecks might well develop as division-sized groupings of troops fly into a relatively few airfields, head off together to collect their equipment from a small number of depots, and adjust to a new environment.[17] Although the Defense Department appears confident, in the absence of a full-scale test it is impossible to foresee how readily prepositioned equipment would support the deployment of nine, six, or even two U.S.-based divisions. For financial and obvious political reasons, however, it is unrealistic to expect such a test.

VULNERABILITY. Many observers, including Hunt and Canby, warn that reinforcement might be disrupted and equipment stockpiles destroyed in the event of delays in the arrival of U.S. troops. Assuming that additional prepositioning is designed to meet the threat of a six-front attack after two weeks' preparation, and that six divisions are to be deployed in ten days and nine in fourteen days, at least six U.S.-based divisions might be deployed at the start of a Warsaw Pact attack if NATO's mobilization lags by four days or less. It appears, however, that only about two divisions would be deployed by the start of this attack if Western mobilization lags by seven days. And in the event of a twelve-day lag, expectations are that all prepositioned equipment would still be sitting in depots at the onset of an attack.

During the mid-1970s, the equipment for about two and a half U.S.-based divisions was stored at three major sites. Richard D. Lawrence and Jeffrey Record criticized the arrangement, warning that it offered "one of the most tempting targets for enemy attention in the entire NATO area"; that the "giant exposed sites" would probably "attract substantial Pact resources aimed at their destruction in the early hours

---

17. Steven Canby, *The Alliance and Europe*, pt. 4: *Military Doctrine and Technology*, Adelphi Paper 109 (London: International Institute for Strategic Studies, 1974), pp. 21–22; Kenneth Hunt, *The Alliance and Europe*, pt. 2: *Defence with Fewer Men*, Adelphi Paper 98 (London: IISS, 1973), p. 41. These analysts recommend that the U.S. Army in Europe be restructured to contain a larger number of divisions that would be fully equipped but only perhaps 75 percent manned in peacetime. These divisions would hold the equipment for U.S.-based reinforcements. They argue that this arrangement would ease the reception of reinforcements and their adjustment, promote better maintenance of the prepositioned equipment, and reduce its vulnerability. While offering several caveats, Hunt argues that such a reorganization would still leave enough fully manned units for initial defense. Canby, *Military Doctrine and Technology*, pp. 21–22; Hunt, *Defence with Fewer Men*, pp. 29–30, 33. The Army, however, has never shown any interest in these proposals.

of a conflict"; and that the storage sites "are vulnerable to air attack, surface-to-surface missile fire, airborne assault, and sabotage."[18] The problem of a relatively small number of storage sites seems to persist. One CBO analyst feels that the current program of prepositioned equipment "involves considerable risk" and that stockpiles "might be vulnerable to destruction by both ground attacks and air strikes." Because equipment has been withdrawn from U.S.-based divisions to increase stocks in Europe, she observes, "reinforcing divisions deployed to Europe would then have considerably less than their authorized level of equipment for combat. Loss of the prepositioned equipment would also create serious deficiencies in the war reserve stockpiles."[19] Some Army officers have privately expressed considerable concern, one going so far as to characterize current prepositioning programs as a "blueprint for disaster."[20] Although the Defense Department has apparently studied the problem of vulnerability of its prepositioned equipment, U.S. officials have not publicly addressed the various concerns.

Thus, while overall flexibility and the readiness of U.S.-based units might suffer somewhat, it appears that additional prepositioning of equipment would improve NATO's prospects against a short-warning six-front attack if NATO responds promptly to warning and if reinforcement goes as planned. Many observers, however, have seriously questioned the wisdom of the prepositioning programs initiated by the Carter administration. Kaufmann, moreover, argues that they were adopted "to a considerable degree because of exaggerated estimates of the Soviet ability to launch surprise attacks with conventional forces."[21]

Additional Forward Deployments

An alternative response to the possibility of a short-warning attack would be the stationing of additional U.S. ground forces in West

18. They warned that current arrangements could invite delays, because the United States might hesitate to fly entire divisions over to pick up equipment in a crisis, for fear of provoking Moscow. Like Hunt and Canby, they favor a restructuring of the U.S. Army in Europe to create a larger number of two-brigade divisions that would each hold the equipment for a third. Among other things, they claim that this arrangement would make it politically and operationally easier to effect rapid reinforcement. Richard D. Lawrence and Jeffrey Record, *U.S. Force Structure in NATO: An Alternative* (Brookings Institution, 1974), pp. 50, 63, 84–86.
19. CBO, *Costs of Prepositioning*, pp. 8–9.
20. Interviews.
21. "The Defense Budget," p. 173.

Germany.[22] A few observers advocate this. William Hyland, a former State Department and National Security Council official, believes that the United States should deploy five additional divisions.[23] Robert Komer, a former under secretary of defense, more modestly recommends that an attack helicopter brigade be stationed in West Germany; presumably, one of its functions would be to serve as the highly mobile element of NATO's operational reserves.[24]

Since some small increases early in the Carter administration, the idea of a further expansion of the American ground presence in West Germany has not attracted much support. Most critics maintain that a substantial increase would be costly, would exacerbate personnel problems, and would encounter political opposition. Hunt points out that "there are no barracks to spare and building new ones would be costly and possibly unwelcome in some locations where it might be operationally desirable to put them."[25] As for American sentiments, it is worth noting that only ten years have passed since Senator Mike Mansfield attracted considerable congressional support for his effort to halve U.S. deployments in Europe.

General objections, criticisms of particular proposals aside, to an increased U.S. contribution would be raised. Some observers believe that the Carter administration placed too much emphasis on programs for NATO's central front. For instance, before becoming assistant secretary of defense for international security affairs, Francis West argued that the Defense Department's "fixation" with "one region of the world distorted both policy and fiscal priorities." One particular view of his—that "on a constrained budget, we must trade off further prepositioned stocks in West Germany in order to have adequate forces beyond NATO"—reflects a belief that "the prime military challenges to U.S. interests lie outside West Germany."[26]

---

22. Richard K. Betts, however, notes that there is no guarantee that forces stationed in the theater would be deployed in a timely manner upon receipt of warning. *Surprise Attack: Lessons for Defense Planning* (Brookings Institution, 1982), pp. 174, 221.

23. Interview.

24. George C. Wilson, *Washington Post*, February 14, 1981. Komer also believes that the United States should plan on using that unit for a Persian Gulf contingency.

25. Kenneth Hunt, "Alternative Conventional Force Postures," in Kenneth A. Myers, ed., *NATO: The Next Thirty Years* (Westview, 1980), pp. 140–41.

26. Francis J. West, Jr., "Conventional Forces Beyond NATO," in Thompson, *National Security in the 1980s*, pp. 330, 336.

Decreasing the U.S. Contribution

Various rationales for reducing the U.S. role in the central front's defense have been advanced. David Calleo, a Johns Hopkins professor, argues that the United States—having taken little or no account of Europe's recovery from the political and economic weakness that warranted the commitment of U.S. forces in 1950—continues to bear a disproportionate share of the burden of European defense.[27] Such arguments are familiar, having been raised in the course of debate over Senator Mansfield's amendments aimed at reducing American troop commitments in Europe. While sensing background sentiment for an updated Mansfield amendment in 1981, Kenneth Adelman suggested—before joining the Reagan administration—that the support for one would emanate from the right instead of the left.[28] Indeed, the events of the late 1970s led some observers to conclude that the United States should reduce its NATO contributions in order to strengthen its capabilities for dealing with what are seen as more pressing threats to vital Western interests elsewhere in the world. William L. Hauser, a former Army officer, colorfully expresses this sentiment: "The American fox has its paws stuck fast to the NATO tarbaby while Soviet-proxy rabbits scamper freely through the third world."[29] Maxwell Taylor, a former chairman of the joint chiefs, also agrees that the United States should orient more of its forces toward threats beyond Europe, both because of the dangers of instability in the third world and because of serious doubts about the viability of plans for the conventional defense of Western Europe.[30] Every proposal for reducing the U.S. contribution to NATO's central front, however, meets with objections.

Reducing Forward Deployments

Some advocates want to reduce the strength of the U.S. Army in Europe to meet requirements elsewhere. Hauser agrees with West that

27. David P. Calleo, "Inflation and American Power," *Foreign Affairs,* vol. 59 (Spring 1981), pp. 805–11.
28. *Wall Street Journal,* April 10, 1981.
29. *New York Times,* February 27, 1981.
30. Maxwell D. Taylor, "Changing Military Priorities," *AEI Foreign Policy and Defense Review,* vol. 1 (April 1979), pp. 4, 8–9.

the United States has sacrificed significant capabilities to intervene elsewhere in order to reinforce NATO; the "Rapid Deployment Force is largely earmarked for wartime duty in Europe, its logistics dependent on unready reserve organizations, its manpower replacement in disarray, and its strategic transport pitifully inadequate." He argues as well that the denial of access to the third world's resources is a more pressing threat to Western security than an invasion of Western Europe, "for the Red Army's Eastern European rear is unreliable, West Germany has superb conventional forces, Britain and France are nuclear powers, and United States escalation is feared by the Soviet Union's planners." Hauser maintains that the United States cannot afford to keep a large force in Europe while simultaneously countering threats in the third world. He believes that "we are already maintaining overstructured, hollow forces that we cannot adequately man, train, keep in repair, or competently control."[31] The "hollow" army assessment echoes one made several months earlier by the Army's chief of staff.[32]

The withdrawal of some U.S. forces from Europe would be consistent with such an assessment. Hauser favors such a course, arguing that "our formations in Europe can be much reduced and still be adequate for deterrence. Europe will (if it must) strengthen its own defenses."[33] Stansfield Turner, a former Sixth Fleet commander and director of the Central Intelligence Agency, proposes a somewhat different response. While indicating that the current number of U.S. forces should remain stationed in Western Europe, he argues that the United States should draw on them rather than units from home for a contingency in Southwest Asia (Komer makes a similar suggestion).[34] Turner points to the higher readiness of U.S. forces in Europe and the fact that they are three times closer to the Middle East. While noting that "our NATO partners would prefer that we take on the Persian Gulf responsibility as an addition to our European posture rather than reducing our forces in Europe," Turner maintains that "we cannot increase the numbers of American forces enough to do that. Consequently, concessions must be made in NATO to permit adequate United States coverage of the Middle East, which is as much in Europe's vital interest as it is in ours."[35]

31. William L. Hauser, *New York Times,* February 27, 1981.
32. Meyer, *White Paper 1980.*
33. William L. Hauser, *New York Times,* February 27, 1981.
34. George C. Wilson, *Washington Post,* February 14, 1981.
35. Stansfield Turner, "Toward A New Defense Strategy," *New York Times Magazine,* May 10, 1981, p. 50.

Reducing Reinforcements

Three assumptions underlie Maxwell Taylor's views regarding U.S. reinforcement of NATO. First, he doubts that the West is prepared to buy the military capability thought needed to contain Soviet military power on the Continent in the event of war. For the United States, this would supposedly entail years of defense expenditures at about 9 percent of GNP.[36] Second, in view of these constraints and "our extensive global obligations elsewhere," Taylor maintains that "our present commitment of ground forces to NATO is already an undesirably large stake." He argues that interference with Western access to third world markets is the most imminent threat, and one that Moscow could safely use to impose its will on the West. Third, while various factors are said to make an invasion relatively unlikely, Taylor insists that the military situation in Europe so favors the Warsaw Pact "as to render highly probable the early defeat of the NATO forces after a short period of intense conventional combat."[37]

All this leads Taylor to conclude, first of all, that it would be "folly" for the United States to send major reinforcements to Europe in a crisis or conflict. Should the United States be "so misguided as to undertake a significant reinforcement of Europe despite the dangers of heavy shipping losses and of destructive bomber/missile attacks on NATO ports and airfields, those forces reaching their destination would have to depend on what remained of an already feeble NATO logistic system inadequate to sustain in combat the troops already there." Taylor worries that the probable loss of the forces committed would cripple the subsequent war-making capability of the United States. While claiming that "these considerations make a strong case for no further increase in the U.S. force contribution to NATO," Taylor holds that improvements in the U.S. and allied forces already deployed in Western Europe "would be well worth a considerable outlay of additional resources." Although pessimistic about the eventual outcome of a conventional war in Europe,

---

36. Taylor, "Changing Military Priorities," pp. 5, 8. The Reagan administration is pushing for substantial increases in defense spending. Its plans for fiscal 1986, however, call for defense to consume just 7 percent of the national product, less than the 9 percent goal suggested by Taylor. Moreover, there is no knowing how long the U.S. consensus behind higher defense spending will last. Finally, the allies have been uneven in their observance of 1977 commitments to effect annual 3 percent real increases in defense spending. See *Wall Street Journal*, February 18, 1981.

37. Taylor, "Changing Military Priorities," pp. 4–5.

Taylor believes that several prospects—in addition to possible escalation—sharply reduce the threat of Soviet attack: heavy losses to Warsaw Pact forces, extensive damage to Western European industry, and the immobilization of sizable forces that might be needed on the Sino-Soviet border. Taylor states that the United States should exploit these factors "to the fullest by concentrating efforts on the improvement of weapons, tactics, troop dispositions, and logistics" of NATO's in-place forces. At the same time, he believes, the United States should expand its general-purpose naval power and maintain a four-division force at home that can rapidly respond to pressing threats elsewhere and sustain combat of moderate intensity for sixty days without major reinforcement. Taylor questions whether the current U.S. force structure, nineteen active and nine reserve divisions, is appropriate.[38]

While Taylor sympathizes with the standard objections to reducing the U.S. contribution to NATO, he maintains that none of them provides a "justification for increasing our human stake in a basically untenable situation [in central Europe] and thus our exposure to losses which would curtail our subsequent ability to help our allies in other ways and places." He believes that NATO's in-place forces should be improved so as to raise their deterrent value. However, his perception of Western Europe's inherent vulnerability to a determined Soviet attack leads Taylor to conclude that "no program to reinforce NATO can be considered adequate."[39]

Reducing Forces

The most radical approach to reducing the U.S. contribution to NATO would be to eliminate some forward-deployed units and some of the home-based units earmarked for NATO from the U.S. force structure. David Calleo favors this course. He argues that America's present troubles stem from an acceleration of domestic inflation and a disintegration of the post-1945 structure of collective security and liberal economic interdependence. Economic policy and geopolitical position, he reasons, have grown so interconnected that "failure in one sphere reverberates in the other." While noting that difficulties at home and abroad have numerous independent causes, Calleo argues that one common contributing factor is an overextension of American resources.

38. Ibid., pp. 4–9.
39. Ibid., p. 11.

His comparison of spending on social and military programs in the advanced industrial democracies leads Calleo to conclude that while American expenditures on the former are not excessive, "by any objective measurement of relative resources the United States plays a disproportionate role in European defense." His discussion points to the disbandment of six U.S. divisions, with two forward-deployed ones apparently included, which would supposedly produce savings of $30 billion within three years. Observing that this "could go a long way toward ending America's regular fiscal deficits," Calleo suggests that "in the coming budgetary battles, with painful domestic sacrifices being called for, potential savings of this magnitude are unlikely to escape notice."[40]

Although the real contributions to NATO security made by each member can be endlessly debated,[41] it is clear that such large U.S. cuts could dramatically change the transatlantic balance of power. Calleo recognizes this and, indeed, suggests a threefold approach for transforming NATO. First, because this is seen as "the most probable way to get the Europeans to take a much larger share of the burden of NATO," the Europeans should be given responsibility for running the alliance. "At the very least, it seems time for a European commander to head NATO. Certainly, the reintegration of French space and arms into the military alliance, if this could be achieved, would in itself be worth several American divisions." Second, the United States should encourage, or at least accept, more powerful and independent allied nuclear forces. Calleo believes that "transformation of the Alliance cannot be limited to its non-nuclear aspects," and that "Soviet-American nuclear parity logically calls for a stronger independent European deterrent." Third, the United States "should stop using Europe's hesitations and divisions as a pretext" for perpetuation of the status quo. "If we grow serious about reducing the cost of our NATO commitment, we must assume that Europe's big powers will act as responsible states and must ourselves not try to prevent them from doing so."[42]

---

40. "Inflation and American Power," pp. 781–82, 805–09.

41. Americans frequently insist that Western Europe does not spend enough on defense. Western Europeans respond with claims that conscription frees them from heavy expenditures on personnel and that the financial, economic, and technical aid they furnish to strategically important countries is usually overlooked. See Kaiser and others, *Western Security,* pp. 12–13, 38–39.

42. Calleo, "Inflation and American Power," pp. 809–11.

This proposed transformation of the alliance would, Calleo admits, entail risk. Moreover, a reduction in the U.S. contribution to NATO's central front would "be only a step toward curing America's inflation, not a panacea." Calleo concludes, however, that without a major decrease in U.S. military expenditures the prospects for controlling inflation seem dim. In that event, "the present frustration of America's domestic and foreign policy may be expected to continue, and transatlantic relations to grow even more acrimonious."[43]

Arguments against any of these proposals for reducing forces are readily available. If the military situation in central Europe is as delicate as chapter 3 portrays it, a significant reduction in the U.S. contribution to NATO could tilt the balance clearly in the Warsaw Pact's favor. In addition, conventional wisdom holds that American reductions could have other destabilizing effects, especially where the West Germans are concerned. Many would agree with the assessment of Fred Iklé, voiced before he became under secretary of defense, that "this could politically be very upsetting to the Germans, where the nervousness comes close to the surface and sometimes above the surface."[44] Western European concern over American military retrenchment raises the specter of a turn either toward militarism or toward neutralism. Although their rightness is debatable, these fears have had a major impact on U.S. defense policy.[45]

Although most observers would agree that military contingencies are most likely to arise outside Europe and that the United States should bear the major responsibility for meeting them, some argue that this should not come at the expense of the American contribution to NATO.[46] Richard Burt, now a State Department official, "would not want a situation to arise where the West and NATO became so weak in the center region that we might be unwilling . . . to react to a problem in the

43. Ibid., p. 811.
44. Thompson, *National Security in the 1980s*, p. 407.
45. Most debate focuses on the possibility of a "finlandization" of Western Europe. See Pierre Hassner, "Detente and Political Change in Europe," *Survival*, vol. 18 (March–April 1976), p. 68; Walter F. Hahn and Robert L. Pfaltzgraff, Jr., eds., *Atlantic Community in Crisis: A Redefinition of the Transatlantic Relationship* (Pergamon, 1979), pp. 193–279. George F. Kennan argues that any analogy with Finland "turns out to be absurdly overdrawn and unsuitable"; "Europe's Problems, Europe's Choices," *Foreign Policy*, Spring 1974, pp. 3–16. It is worth noting that even the cost-conscious Eisenhower administration did not significantly reduce U.S. forces in Europe.
46. In this study, four divisions are assumed to be needed to respond to a Persian Gulf contingency because that is the force the Defense Department postulates for planning purposes.

gulf for fear that it might trigger Soviet military pressure in Central Europe."[47] Others worry that the use of U.S. forces based in Europe for a Middle East contingency—an option favored by Turner and Komer—could widen such a conflict to include Europe. The four foreign affairs council directors acknowledge the West's "obvious interest in maintaining an option of limiting any possible military conflict between East and West to the Middle East, and of preventing its automatic spill-over to Europe." They argue that the West should have enough additional forces to cover other regions so that it would not automatically have to use forces stationed in Europe.[48]

Redirecting the U.S. Contribution

Instead of favoring straightforward increases or decreases in the resources provided, some analysts want to change the way in which the U.S. contribution to NATO's central front is allocated. They believe that improper appreciation for the true nature of the threat has somehow produced an inappropriate allocation of American defense expenditures. Steven Canby and others argue that the U.S. Army has never come to grips with Soviet organizational and warfighting concepts. Taking a different perspective, William Kaufmann maintains that the United States tends to overestimate the speed with which the Warsaw Pact could organize a major attack.

From Support to Combat Capability

Many analysts—Canby being the most prominent—have long argued for redirecting a substantial portion of Army manpower from support to combat units.[49] Usually they note that division slices for the U.S. Army in Europe amount to about 34,600 men and for Soviet forces deployed in Eastern Europe to only about 17,500.[50] Yet, the tank and artillery

---

47. Thompson, *National Security in the 1980s*, p. 409.
48. Kaiser and others, *Western Security*, p. 33.
49. Discussion here focuses on Canby's arguments. See also William S. Lind, "Some Doctrinal Questions for the United States Army," *Military Review*, vol. 57 (March 1977), pp. 54–65; Edward N. Luttwak, "The American Style of Warfare and the Military Balance," *Survival*, vol. 21 (March–April 1979), pp. 57–60.
50. A division slice is a division plus a proportionate share of the nondivisional troops and administrative overhead for a given force. International Institute for Strategic

holdings of the latter are roughly comparable to those of their American counterparts. The Warsaw Pact division slice contains fewer support assets. Warsaw Pact forces are supposed to win before logistical deficiencies become a problem, usually by attempting to overwhelm opposing defenses through massed breakthrough attacks. Canby argues that U.S. (and allied) forces are inappropriately structured to meet this threat. He believes that NATO would not have enough forces (particularly in its operational reserves), that a short war would require fewer maintenance and supply assets than are now available, that units outside sectors targeted for breakthroughs would not need a full complement of organic support, and that expeditionary trappings are unnecessary in a region like Western Europe where civil-sector resources (fuel, communications, hospitals, and so forth) might be drawn upon. Through the streamlining of existing forces and the pooling of residual logistical assets, which would in wartime be directed toward hard-pressed units, Canby believes that division slices of 20,000 men each would be attainable and perfectly adequate. The men freed by such measures could be used to create additional active combat formations or to provide cadres for reserve units. Canby maintains that the structure of the U.S. Army in Europe should accordingly be changed from two armored cavalry regiments, three forward-deployed brigades, and four divisions to nine divisions, two armored cavalry regiments, and a number of independent maneuver battalions. In theory, this new force could be equipped with some of the materiel already deployed, prepositioned, or stockpiled for war reserve.[51] While the availability of additional forces would initially improve NATO's prospects for combatting short-warning or reinforced attacks, the impact of such a reorganization on the Army's staying power would be substantial.

Such arguments and proposals have inspired some changes, but they have also met with criticism and institutional resistance. Beliefs that another European war would be short and that the U.S. Army's tooth-to-tail ratio should accordingly be adjusted upward did prompt 1974 legislation to replace 18,000 support personnel with combat personnel, including those for two brigades dispatched in 1975 and 1976. Many Army officers complain that these cuts went too far, however, and left

---

Studies, *The Military Balance, 1980–1981* (London: IISS, 1980), p. 6; *1977–1978*, p. 110. The U.S. Army in Europe's 3 brigades and 2 cavalry regiments are counted in this study as 1⅔ divisions.

51. Canby, *Military Doctrine and Technology*, pp. 18–19, 21.

the Army with insufficient staying power.[52] One former Army commander argues that increases in the intensity of combat—to levels like those experienced in the 1973 Middle East war—could more than offset any decrease in a war's likely duration, that a European war might become protracted, and that greater reliance on host-nation support would be imprudent.[53] Thus, the merits of wholesale conversions of tail into teeth are debatable. Since "it has not been demonstrated convincingly that the Soviet emphasis on ready combat-power as opposed to sustained combat capability . . . [is] preferable to American priorities," defense consultant Edward N. Luttwak sees "a *prima facie* case against the great strains and costs of such a reorganization."[54] A break with traditional ways of doing business would naturally be discomforting. Memories of World War II, when it received assured logistical support in every theater of operations,[55] would presumably leave the Army reluctant to adopt a Soviet-style support structure. It is also doubtful that the Army would readily prune its divisions and reorganize them along Soviet lines.[56] The current organizational pattern of U.S. Army divisions goes back at least to the reorganization of 1939–41, as Canby notes. He himself admits that adoption of his proposed changes would be "wrenching" for the organizations involved.[57] Whatever the intellectual merits of the arguments for such a change, it thus appears that a drastic restructuring of the U.S. Army is not going to occur anytime soon.

52. The 1974–76 reduction of U.S. division slices from 38,000 to 33,500 men drew complaints from many officers. See quote from a 1978 speech by the Army chief of staff in Brig. Gen. William G. P. Tuttle, Jr., USA, "Combat Service Support: Rusty Blade Behind the Cutting Edge," *Army*, vol. 29 (August 1979), p. 19. For detailed discussions of claimed shortfalls in the U.S. support capability, see Maj. John G. Zierdt, Jr., USA, "Firepower, Not Troops, Key to 'Tooth' Strength," *Army*, vol. 29 (June 1979), pp. 55–56; "America's 'Hollow Army' in Europe," *International Defense Review*, vol. 14, no. 3 (1981), pp. 242–43.

53. Gen. James H. Polk, USA (ret.), "The New Short War Strategy," *Strategic Review*, vol. 3 (Summer 1975), pp. 52–56.

54. "Perceptions of Military Force and U.S. Defense Policy," *Survival*, vol. 19 (January–February 1977), p. 2.

55. Russell F. Weigley, *History of the United States Army* (Macmillan, 1967), p. 479.

56. The Army, in fact, now plans on raising the size of its heavy divisions to include almost 20,000 men. See Maj. Paul A. Bigelman, USA, "Force Designs for the Future," *Army*, vol. 31 (June 1981), pp. 22–26, 29–30, 33.

57. Steven L. Canby, *Short (And Long) War Responses: Restructuring, Border Defense, and Reserve Mobilization for Armored Warfare*, prepared for U.S. Department of Defense, Director of Special Studies (Santa Monica, Calif.: Technology Service Corp., 1978), pp. 18, 40.

From Rapid to Deliberate Reinforcement

Some analysts would like to see the United States deemphasize rapid reinforcement in favor of plans for a more deliberate reinforcement of central Europe. They argue that the procurement of additional ships and increases in reserve readiness would enable the United States after several weeks to deliver more forces of higher readiness than it now could, albeit at some sacrifice of earlier deployments.

Kaufmann would not object to the prepositioning of additional equipment for U.S.-based divisions and the procurement of new heavy cargo aircraft, which are now looked to as hedges against short-warning attack. But he maintains that the procurement of additional sealift facilities and the full equipping of more reserve units should come first since he is dubious of the Warsaw Pact's capacity for quickly organizing a major attack and of the practicability of rapid reinforcement through airlift and prepositioning. Claiming that sealift is cheaper and more reliable, Kaufmann argues that the United States should hold off on the C-X cargo aircraft and instead procure forty-eight fast cargo ships at a cost of about $5.9 billion.[58] Secretary Brown indicated that eight of these thirty-three-knot ships could deliver a heavy division plus some nondivisional support and initial supplies to the central front in fifteen days.[59] It thus appears that Kaufmann's proposal might conceivably permit deployment of the equivalent of twelve additional divisions during the first thirty days of mobilization. Citing the possibility of a tardy NATO response to warning, Kaufmann admits that sealift "might prove too slow."[60] Maxwell Taylor and others, however, worry at least as much about the security of ships en route and attacks on debarkation points in an early outbreak of hostilities.[61]

If strategic mobility is to be improved to allow for the earlier deployment of reserve component units, then something must also be done to improve the readiness of these forces. Hence, Kaufmann also argues that equipment now earmarked for additional prepositioning should instead go to alleviate equipment shortages within the reserve compo-

58. "The Defense Budget," pp. 173, 176.
59. *Department of Defense Annual Report, Fiscal Year 1982*, p. 203.
60. "The Defense Budget," p. 173.
61. Taylor, "Changing Military Priorities"; also see Paul H. Nitze and others, *Securing the Seas: The Soviet Naval Challenge and Western Alliance Options* (Westview, 1979), pp. 86, 88, 93, 111, 157–58, 161–62, 195–96, 199–200, 337–82.

nents.[62] Even fully equipped and manned reserve units—personnel shortfalls also being a current problem[63]—would need time after mobilization for training to achieve full combat readiness. Experts agree that training requirements would vary with the size of a reserve unit, but their estimates of the time needed for training differ. While companies should need no additional training after mobilization, Martin Binkin indicates that the shakedown time for the integration of reserve companies into active battalions could amount to two weeks, of reserve battalions into active brigades six weeks, and of reserve brigades into active divisions ten weeks; fourteen weeks would be needed to prepare divisions wholly unmanned in peacetime.[64] According to Fischer, this has in part to do with the establishment of command and control between successively higher echelons. Indeed, while maintaining that reserve units at the battalion level can be kept ready for mobilization, he suggests that at the brigade level, cadred reserve units that possess at least a skeleton command structure in peacetime can also be kept ready. It appears that the reserve battalions and brigades assigned to round out active U.S. divisions maintain higher readiness than Binkin's figures would suggest.

Several schemes for reducing postmobilization training requirements through closer integration of the Army's active and reserve components have been proposed or tried. Ned Sabrosky, a manpower analyst, proposes a transfer of some active-duty personnel from regular divisions to provide active cadres for National Guard divisions. Currently, the Army employs just over fourteen divisions' worth of active-duty personnel to man twenty-four active and reserve divisions; twelve are manned at 90–100 percent strength, four at about 70 percent, and eight are wholly unmanned until mobilization. Sabrosky suggests that eight divisions be 100 percent manned and immediately available; eight be 50 percent manned and available after three to four days; and eight be 25 percent manned in peacetime and available after four to six weeks.[65] This

62. "The Defense Budget," p. 174.
63. See Maj. Gen. William R. Berkman, USA, "Reserves: Expanded Missions, Limited Resources," *Army,* vol. 30 (October 1980), pp. 166–69.
64. *U.S. Reserve Forces: The Problem of the Weekend Warrior* (Brookings Institution, 1974), pp. 10, 45, 46.
65. The 50 percent manned divisions would integrate reserve companies into active battalions, while the 25 percent would integrate battalions into brigades. Alan Ned Sabrosky, "U.S. General Purpose Forces: Four Essential Reforms," *Orbis,* vol. 24 (Fall 1980), pp. 514, 522–27.

arrangement, which its proponent considers politically and militarily adequate, is meant to improve the readiness of later-deploying reserve divisions, make it easier for the Army to meet its active manpower targets, and free some resources for U.S. naval, air, and strategic mobility forces through a slight reduction in active-duty Army manpower.[66] The readiness of eight regular divisions would be lowered in return for an increase in the readiness of eight reserve divisions. Some Defense Department analysts have also favored the assignment of active cadres to some National Guard divisions.[67] The Army, however, has never demonstrated any interest in such an arrangement.

Expansion of reserve affiliation programs provides another path to closer integration of the Army's active and reserve components. The Army's current program for using reserve units to augment full-strength divisions reflects a belief that divisions can accommodate more subordinate units than they are normally assigned in peacetime. Experience indicates that a division is capable of controlling four as opposed to three brigades, while a brigade has a capacity for managing five instead of just two to four battalions.[68] Although it appears that the eighteen U.S. divisions earmarked for deployment in Europe ninety days after mobilization begins would be joined by sixteen separate brigades, only four brigades—as well as two maneuver battalions—are now officially designated as augmentation units.[69] This suggests that the potential exists for assigning more reserve units to the augmentation role, one form of active-reserve affiliation. The director of the Army National Guard (ARNG) maintains that affiliation "continues to be an outstanding vehicle for improving the readiness of ARNG units through dedicated support and assistance of active units."[70]

Rounding out understrength divisions with reserve units is another form of affiliation. Four brigades and ten maneuver battalions are now so assigned.[71] The Army appears reasonably satisfied with this program. Indeed, its chief of staff feels that to retain sixteen active divisions and accommodate their planned reorganization, the Army must consider

66. Ibid.
67. Michael Getler, *Washington Post*, June 7, 1973.
68. *Annual Defense Department Report, FY1975*, p. 100; *Annual Defense Department Report, FY1976 and FY197T*, p. III/42.
69. Maj. Gen. Emmett H. Walker, Jr., USA, "Progress in Training, Readiness, Manning," *Army*, vol. 30 (October 1980), p. 154.
70. Ibid., p. 153.
71. Ibid., p. 154; Berkman, "Reserves," p. 166.

more widespread use of reserve companies, battalions, or brigades to round out regular divisions. General Meyer maintains that U.S.-based units, with the exception of rapid deployment forces, "may have to be structured with a mix of active strength and reserve strength keyed to their deployment sequence."[72] The Army's willingness to consider this step may in part be a response to the increasingly tight manpower forecasts for the 1980s.[73] Greater reliance on reserve units to augment or round out active forces would presumably allow the Army to get by with fewer active-duty personnel than would otherwise be needed. This would make it easier for the Army to meet its manpower goals in an all-volunteer environment.

A redirection of resources toward sealift and reserve forces might well increase the number and readiness of the units that the United States could deploy in central Europe after several weeks of mobilization. In return, however, the United States would sacrifice some of its current capability for reinforcing NATO during the first few weeks of mobilization. Hence, proposals for such redirection would arouse criticism from those concerned with the possibility of a short-warning attack. While Kaufmann maintains that the Warsaw Pact's ability to launch surprise attacks with conventional forces has been exaggerated, he worries that NATO might not respond to available warning in a timely manner. In either case, deliberate reinforcement might prove too slow. Kaufmann suggests, however, that "if the allies are concerned about the time it takes to deliver [U.S.] reinforcements, they can always provide more of the high-readiness, early-deploying forces themselves."[74]

Looking to the Allies

There is fairly widespread agreement among American observers that Western Europe should improve its ground force capabilities. It is felt that this would leave NATO with higher confidence in its ability to defend the central front in a conventional war, especially if substantial

---

72. Meyer, *White Paper 1980*, p. 3.
73. Taking 1979 as a base year, the number of 18-year-old males is projected to decline 16 percent by 1985 and 26 percent by 1992. U.S. Census Bureau, *Projections of the Population of the United States: 1975 to 2050*, Current Population Reports, series P-25, no. 601 (GPO, 1975), pp. 45–58.
74. "The Defense Budget," p. 173.

86 *Defense of Central Europe*

U.S. reinforcements had to be diverted to one or more contingencies outside NATO. Four paths to improvement have been suggested: additional deployments in West Germany of existing active forces; establishment of additional active forces; improvements in mobilization capabilities of European forces; and preparation of defensive positions in peacetime.

Additional Forward Deployments

The disposition of certain allied forces has been a source of some concern. During the 1970s, Belgium brought home two of the four brigades it had stationed in West Germany. The British Army of the Rhine has continuously had to provide some troops on a rotating basis for Northern Ireland. Although the army's nominal strength has remained at 55,000 men, the government is reportedly considering a permanent return of 2,000–3,000 headquarters and communications personnel to Britain.[75] Between 1976 and 1980, the number of French troops in West Germany decreased from 58,000 to 47,000.[76] The number of Dutch troops in West Germany also declined, although the Netherlands has kept one brigade deployed forward. This brigade could not, however, adequately cover the sixty-kilometer-wide Dutch corps sector, and an attack on it before the arrival of Dutch reinforcements (five active and three to four reserve brigades) would probably result in a breakthrough.

In their 1977 report, Senators Nunn and Bartlett indicated that they would favor additional allied deployments in West Germany. Most of their discussion focused on the danger of a short-warning attack. They argued that this threat "greatly magnifies the importance of forces *already* in place on the Continent, the bulk of which are and of necessity must be European." "At a minimum," the senators maintained, "Allied contributions to the defense of NATO Center should be stabilized and improved both in strength and location."[77]

The deployment forward of additional allied forces would entail some expense, such as balance-of-payments costs, which might or might not be offset by the West German government. There would also be

75. Drew Middleton, *New York Times*, May 19, 1981.
76. IISS, *Military Balance, 1976–1977*, p. 22; *1980–1981*, p. 25.
77. Senator Sam Nunn and Senator Dewey F. Bartlett, *NATO and the New Soviet Threat*, a report to the Senate Armed Services Committee, 95 Cong. 1 sess. (GPO, 1977), pp. 10–11.

construction, transportation, and other relocation costs. While admitting that they would reduce the time required for movement to wartime positions, a former inspector general of the West German Army argues that additional forward deployments would not be worth their cost. General de Maiziere maintains that, apart from not producing any new combat power, additional forward deployments could hinder equipment modernization by reducing the capital investment portion of various defense budgets.[78] The implicit assumption here is that NATO would have enough warning and respond quickly enough for the active forces of certain allies to move hundreds of kilometers before the onset of hostilities.

Additional Active Forces

When people talk of an increase in active allied forces, they usually mean West German. Proportionally, a number of NATO countries spend more on defense or keep more men under arms—some, like the United States, doing both—than does West Germany.[79] Were it to maintain as large a proportion of men under arms as does the United States, West Germany could create perhaps another ten active brigades.[80] By adding within three days of mobilization another 40,000 men in major combat units to NATO's combat potential, this step could significantly improve the prospects for containing a short-warning attack.

Conventional wisdom, however, has long held that an expansion of the West German Army might well prove destabilizing. Most of the limits placed on West German forces and armaments in agreements reached after World War II still stand.[81] A former State Department official, Leon Sloss, holds the typical view that West Germany "must

78. Gen. Ulrich de Maiziere, GA (ret.), "Rational Deployment of Forces on the Central Front," study prepared for the Assembly of the Western European Union, April 2, 1975, pp. 30–31.
79. IISS, *Military Balance, 1979–1980*, pp. 94, 96.
80. Currently, 0.92 percent of the U.S. population serves on active duty. Application of that percentage to West Germany's population would provide 72,000 additional men. If current practices were followed, just under 60 percent would be assigned to combat units; IISS, *Military Balance, 1980–1981*, pp. vii, 26.
81. These included a limitation of 500,000 men on the size of its military, a prohibition on chemical or nuclear arms, and restrictions on warship construction. In July 1980, however, the Western European Union canceled all restraints on West German shipbuilding. Bonn also abandoned a self-imposed limit on naval deployments beyond 24 hours' sailing distance from the Danish straits. Thomas Ries, "Expanding Horizons for the Bundesmarine," *International Defense Review*, vol. 13, no. 7 (1980), p. 986.

maintain a relatively low profile to avoid antagonizing the Russians or alarming its allies."[82] One U.S. Army officer argues, however, that the societies of Nazi Germany and the Federal Republic should be recognized as fundamentally different, that Soviet fears of West Germany should not be exaggerated, that Bonn's assumption of a leadership role would produce a healthier Atlantic community, and that "modest" growth in the West German Army should be politically acceptable. Colonel Vardamis goes on to suggest that a plan for expanding the West German Army might have the politically desirable effect of making Moscow eager to reach an agreement on reductions of conventional forces in central Europe.[83] The political and military repercussions from an increase in the size of Bonn's army cannot, however, be predicted with any confidence. For its part, the West German government is far from contemplating any increase in active strength. It remains sensitive to external concerns about West Germany's military capabilities, critical of what it regards as simple-minded comparisons based on total population and national income, cognizant of a coming decline in numbers of young men, and reluctant for the time being to program significant increases in defense spending.[84]

Improved Mobilization Capabilities

The creation of additional reserve combat units is the most favored option for augmenting allied ground capabilities. Events in Southwest Asia during the late 1970s heightened support for improvements in Western Europe's mobilization capabilities. The Carter administration reportedly urged the allies to organize as many as ten new reserve brigades, which could fill in should U.S. reinforcements have to be diverted to the Persian Gulf.[85]

Years before that, however, such analysts as Hunt and Canby pointed to the untapped mobilization potential of West Germany, France,

82. *NATO Reform: Prospects and Priorities*, Georgetown University, Center for Strategic and International Studies, Washington Papers, vol. 3, no. 30 (Sage, 1975), p. 26.

83. Alex A. Vardamis, "German-American Military Fissures," *Foreign Policy*, Spring 1979, pp. 87–106.

84. See West German Minister of Defense, *White Paper 1975–1976: The Security of the Federal Republic of Germany and the Development of the Federal Armed Forces* (Federal Minister of Defense, 1976), pp. 82–83, and *White Paper 1979*, pp. 150–51, 226; John Vinocur, *New York Times*, November 13, 1980; December 18, 1981.

85. John Fialka, *Washington Star*, April 24, 1980.

Table 4-1. Reserve Establishments of Belgium, France, the Netherlands, and West Germany, 1980

| Country | Trained army reservists | Major reserve combat units | | Other reservists |
		Composition	Number of reservists	
Belgium	111,000	2 brigades	7,000	104,000
France	280,000	10 divisions[a]	69,000	211,000
Netherlands	145,000	4 brigades[b]	15,000	130,000
West Germany	590,000[c]	21 brigades and regiments	67,000	523,000
Total	1,126,000	. . .	158,000	968,000

Source: International Institute for Strategic Studies, *The Military Balance, 1980–1981* (London: IISS, 1980), pp. 21, 25, 26–27, 29–30. See also West German Minister of Defense, *White Paper 1979: The Security of the Federal Republic of Germany and the Development of the Armed Forces* (Federal Minister of Defense, 1979), pp. 150, 155.
a. Trainees at military schools would form another 4 divisions.
b. An undisclosed number of additional infantry brigades could be mobilized for home defense.
c. Estimate.

Belgium, and the Netherlands.[86] Each year, their military establishments release about a half-million conscripts after eight to seventeen months' service.[87] The reserve establishments of these countries contain over one million men, yet they have so few major combat units that only about 158,000 reservists would serve in them (see table 4-1). Some of the other reservists would be used to round out active divisions or, as in the case of West Germany, would be assigned to rear-area security or nondivisional support units. It appears, however, that a huge number of trained reservists are assigned to individual replacement pools rather than organized units. Canby attributes this to NATO's adoption of Anglo-American preferences for individual replacement, the supreme headquarters' fear that emphasis on anything other than expensive standing forces would encourage shirking by member countries, Western Europe's traditional emphasis on nuclear deterrence, and the influence of U.S. military skepticism about the value of reserve forces. He suggests that a comparison of today's reserve establishments with those activated by the continental countries at the onset of World War II indicates their mobilization potential as well as a "conceptual and organizational malaise" within NATO.[88] This indictment accompanies an assertion that

86. For instance, see Hunt's 1973 study, *Defence With Fewer Men*, pp. 25–26.
87. The total for just the four armies in 1980 was about 406,000; estimate based on IISS, *Military Balance, 1980–1981*, pp. 21, 25–27, 29–30.
88. Canby, *Short (And Long) War Responses*, p. 88. In September 1939, Germany deployed 98 divisions (52 active and 46 reserve) and France deployed 110 (65 active and 45 reserve). Belgium mobilized 700,000 men in January 1940, and 1 million by May 1940. The Netherlands mobilized 14 divisions in January 1940.

the annual release of another half-million trained conscripts means that "Western Europe has the wherewithal to create the forces necessary for its own defense."[89]

Additional reserve units, while cheaper than active units, would require extra outlays for training, perhaps for a few civilian technicians and active-duty cadres, and for equipment. It is difficult to say how much. Sloss notes that ongoing modernization programs should release older equipment perhaps suitable for reserve use.[90] This has indeed been the principal source of equipment for combat units in West Germany's Territorial Army. The Dutch Army reportedly places annual expenditures—apparently including equipment amortization—on its reserve units at about 20 percent of those for their active counterparts.[91] Canby maintains that additional reserve units could in many cases be used as blocking, antitank infantry, whose simple equipment, few peacetime personnel, and minimal training requirements would cost only about 10 percent of the amount spent on high-quality active units. Indeed, he claims that Western Europe could triple its division count for increases of only 30 percent in its army budgets and 15 percent in its overall defense budget.[92] Western European governments, however, are reluctant to program any substantial rise in defense spending. Hence, some observers believe that alliance responsibilities would need to be reallocated to free resources for a major increase in the number of combat units in the reserve establishments of continental armies.

89. Ibid. In suggesting how additional units might be organized, Hunt talks about using reserve combat units to round out active forces; "Alternative Conventional Force Postures," p. 143. Canby, *Military Doctrine and Technology,* pp. 20–21, originally focused on restructuring continental armies to create smaller peacetime division slices, thereby freeing personnel to serve as active cadres for reserve units; he suggested that the four continental countries could, within existing active and reserve strengths, create 60 divisions, and that 15 might be 100 percent manned in peacetime, 20 be 50 percent manned, and 25 be 25 percent manned. Resistance to such proposals has apparently led Canby to favor more widespread use of the Dutch system of direct mobilization; see *Short (And Long) War Responses,* pp. 86, 91–93. As Hunt ("Alternative Conventional Force Postures," p. 144) puts it, "this system replicates active units by placing entire units, complete with their equipment, on a period of leave equal to and immediately after their initial training time, which is added to their military service."

90. *NATO Reform,* p. 41.

91. Canby, *Short (And Long) War Responses,* p. 93.

92. Ibid., pp. 95–96. Canby assumes that half the additional divisions would be mobile formations (at 20 percent cost) and the other half antitank infantry (at 10 percent cost). Ground forces are said to account for 50 percent of Western Europe's defense spending. Unfortunately, there are no data available to assess these estimates.

Should the U.S. Contribution Change? 91

The lower cost of reserve forces reflects, not surprisingly, their generally lower quality. Indeed, the defense consultant Phillip Karber doubts the ability of militiamen or reservists to maintain their weapons and an adequate level of military proficiency.[93] The British Army's commander foresees command and control problems and dismisses the possibility of reservists indulging in a form of guerrilla antitank warfare.[94] No one seriously believes that lightly armed reserve forces could long withstand attacks by heavy Warsaw Pact formations. Mainstream proponents of improvements in Western Europe's mobilization capabilities, however, typically refrain from extravagant claims for territorial or reserve forces. They reject proposals, which frequently evoke visions of West Germany's transformation into a gigantic hornet's nest, for basing the defense of Western Europe on the Swiss or Yugoslav model.[95] Stressing simplicity in missions, organization, and equipment, they admit that lower-quality reserve units could operate only in secondary sectors and special terrain, and only as adjuncts to regular forces. However, Canby believes that reserve or territorial units, by holding built-up localities within open areas or operating within the 20 to 50+ percent of the region where the terrain is suitable for infantry operations, could make several valuable contributions. Most important, he and Hunt both feel that the availability of additional reserves for defensive tasks in certain areas would free some portion of NATO's expensive regular forces to concentrate elsewhere, either as forward defenders in open corridors or as operational reserves.[96] Even skeptics admit that additional reserve units, despite light armament, would be better than nothing.[97] For their part, the West Germans plan to organize an additional

---

93. Phillip A. Karber, *Force Restructuring and New Weapons Technologies: Relationships in NATO Armies & Operations* (McLean, Va.: BDM Corp., 1978), p.77.

94. Gen. Sir William Scotter, "A Role for Non-Mechanised Infantry," *Journal of the Royal United Services Institute for Defence Studies*, vol. 125 (December 1980), p. 61.

95. According to one Rand analyst, "what is at issue is not the complete substitution of such forces for standing strike forces, but . . . some shift in defense structure from standing strike forces to territorial forces." Horst Mendershausen, *Territorial Defense in NATO and Non-NATO Europe*, R-1184-ISA, prepared for U.S. Department of Defense, Office of the Assistant Secretary of Defense/International Security (Santa Monica, Calif.: Rand Corp., 1973), p. 22.

96. Canby, *Short (And Long) War Responses,* pp. 55–56; Hunt, "Alternative Conventional Force Postures," pp. 143–44.

97. Interviews.

three heavy and three light home defense regiments by the mid-1980s.[98] Conceivably, they might be willing to create more if more resources were available.

The creation of additional reserve forces, Sloss admits, would probably mean a higher and possibly unsettling military profile for West Germany. He draws attention, however, to the combined mobilization potential of its Western neighbors,[99] which table 4-1 indicates almost equals that of West Germany. As for Eastern perceptions, advocates of improved mobilization capabilities typically characterize reserve forces—lightly armed territorials in particular—as an "inoffensive deterrent."[100] In any case, Sloss argues that "the time has come for NATO to reassess its mobilization plans, to decide whether it can afford, in present circumstances, the luxury of letting such political factors detract from its defense capabilities."[101] The apparently inoffensive nature of reserve forces could, Betts suggests, have the benefit of facilitating response to warning.[102] This would significantly improve NATO's prospects for meeting the attacks posited in chapter 3. It is argued that NATO would be less reluctant to respond to a crisis by deploying light reserve units to the border than heavy forces—which some might see as provocative. Some might dismiss this point, but it is difficult to disagree with Hunt that "the European allies are obviously geographically placed to mobilize and move [reserve] forces rapidly."[103] Sloss's only real concern seems to be that "greater reliance on reserve forces could become simply a rationalization for saving money at the expense of an adequate military balance."[104] Mendershausen and Canby suggest, however, that this concern has served in the past as a rationalization for not putting Western Europe's large reserve manpower pool to what is seen as a good use.[105]

Thus, there seems to be general agreement that additional allied reserve forces would be useful. Canby is the most enthusiastic advocate and, indeed, suggests that the allies should organize enough reserve

98. In 1979, West Germany announced that it would add 6 heavy and 6 light home defense regiments by the mid-1980s; West German Minister of Defense, *White Paper 1979*, pp. 154–56. In tables 3-3 and 3-4 it is assumed that this program is half complete.
99. *NATO Reform*, pp. 40–41.
100. Mendershausen, *Territorial Defense in NATO*, pp. 98–99.
101. *NATO Reform*, p. 41.
102. *Surprise Attack*, pp. 174, 221.
103. "Alternative Conventional Force Postures," p. 144.
104. *NATO Reform*, p. 42.
105. See Mendershausen, *Territorial Defense in NATO*, pp. 5, 31, 98–99. See also note 88, above.

combat units to double or triple their total division count.[106] Although this would presumably provide NATO with a comfortable cushion on its central front, no such program appears in the offing. West Germany is planning a modest increase in its number of home defense units. While many observers believe that the organization of still more reserve forces would provide some increase in NATO's confidence in its defensive capabilities and some insurance against any diversion of U.S. reinforcements to other contingencies, most see the costs involved as a serious obstacle.

Defensive Preparations

Many observers have suggested that the peacetime construction of some defensive positions and preparation of some terrain would make the West German border more defendable.[107] Hunt, for one, believes that the manning of static positions would be a useful task within the capability of reserve forces.[108] The most detailed proposal for defensive preparations to appear in recent years comes from John Tillson, a Defense Department official who formerly commanded armored cavalry. He believes that NATO's current forward defense plans invite penetration and encirclement, that NATO cannot count on enough warning to prepare positions after mobilization, that it must employ the high-quality forces available to the best possible use, and that its reserve forces should be assigned relatively simple tasks. He argues for the creation of a forty-kilometer-wide defensive zone along West Germany's border. (To create prepared defenses to this depth would take about thirty days.) Tillson suggests spending perhaps $3 billion over three to five years on special landscaping (afforestation, walled terraces, water obstacles, hedgerows); preparation of bridges, roads, and railways for emergency demolition; and emplacement of numerous protective positions from which to observe and cover obstacles. Through the extensive use of reservists to help man this zone, some of NATO's expensive regular forces would be freed to form mobile reserves, one of the major benefits claimed for this proposal.[109]

106. *Short (And Long) War Responses,* pp. 86, 89, 95–96.
107. For instance, see Michael Howard, "NATO and the Year of Europe," *Survival,* vol. 16 (January–February 1974), p. 26; Kaufmann, "The Defense Budget," p. 173.
108. "Alternative Conventional Force Postures," p. 144.
109. John C. F. Tillson, "The Forward Defense of Europe," ACIS Research Note 5 (UCLA Center for International and Strategic Affairs, 1979), pp. 1–15.

94 Defense of Central Europe

Those who object to such proposals on military grounds typically cite the Maginot Line as proof of the futility of prepared defenses. This is hardly fair, since the German attack of 1940—rather than attempting a direct penetration—outflanked the line by moving via Belgium across an unfortified section of the French frontier.[110] Most observers would agree, however, with General de Maiziere that an attacker can always break through at some point in any barrier by concentrating enough forces,[111] and with Omar Bradley that a fixed defensive line "becomes useless" without mobile reserves. If used, however, to blunt an assault and buy time for the defense to assemble reserves and launch a counterattack, "the concrete fortifications of a fixed defensive line can be worth many divisions," according to General Bradley.[112] Citing U.S. Army findings that obstacles and defensive positions can produce a 500 to 1,000 percent increase in the defensive effectiveness of direct fire weapons, Tillson feels "it is clear that such preparations can significantly enhance a defender's capability." He also claims that prepared defenses would delay an attacker, a prospect likely to disturb Soviet planners intent on quick victory, and buy time for counterattacks.[113] Indeed, Trevor Dupuy's historical studies suggest that an encounter with prepared rather than hasty defenses could be expected to cut an attacker's advance rate by half.[114] For their part, the Israelis feel that fortifications and other preparations were a great help on the Golan front in the 1973 war.[115] A final objection offered by de Maiziere is that mobile forces that would otherwise be available for use as operational reserves would have to be assigned to any defensive zone.[116] This view, however, contradicts the traditional portrayal of defensive preparations as an economy-of-force measure designed, above all, to free forces for inclusion in an operational reserve. Tillson takes this concept a step further by suggesting that reserve forces that can be rapidly mobilized should be given primary

110. B. H. Liddell Hart, *History of the Second World War* (Putnam, 1970), pp. 35, 41, 69, 241.
111. "Rational Deployment of Forces," p. 38.
112. Omar N. Bradley, *A Soldier's Story* (Holt, 1951), p. 243.
113. Tillson, "Forward Defense of Europe," pp. 5–7.
114. Colonel T. N. Dupuy, *Numbers, Predictions, and War: Using History to Evaluate Combat Factors and Predict the Outcome of Battles* (Bobbs-Merrill, 1979), p. 211.
115. Chaim Herzog, *The War of Atonement: October, 1973* (Little, Brown, 1975), pp. 113–14. For an explanation of why Israeli preparations on the Sinai front did not work as well as they might have, see p. 181.
116. "Rational Deployment of Forces," p. 38.

responsibility for manning static defenses, so as to free more of NATO's well-trained mechanized forces to perform the more demanding counterattack role.[117]

Political objections to the peacetime construction of defensive positions would apparently be more difficult to overcome. Conventional wisdom holds that West Germany would never agree to preparing defenses along its eastern border. It is commonly assumed that Bonn would not want to arouse domestic opposition, or cement the division of Germany, or upset the Russians or East Germans. But Tillson insists that "the question of NATO's defensive capability should override" such considerations.[118] He believes that military construction in border areas need not be overly disruptive and that "if the Germans are serious about defending with minimum loss of territory and if defensive preparations are pursued with care over a period of years, the West German government should be able to overcome the objections of the border area residents."[119] As for objections to recognizing the existence of two German states, Tillson argues that Bonn has already implicitly granted de facto recognition through its *Ostpolitik*.[120] In this regard, one could mention as well Bonn's accession to the Helsinki Final Act of the Conference on Security and Cooperation in Europe. Finally, Tillson discounts suggestions that preparing defensive positions would be more provocative "than maintaining standing forces oriented to the east."[121] Indeed, although critical of proposals for a defensive barrier, de Maiziere notes that while giving "evidence—which can be overlooked by neither friend nor foe—of the implementation of the requirement for a forward defence," the creation of "a barrier mainly armed with defensive weapons would make evident . . . the deliberate limitation of NATO to defence."[122] Betts agrees that the existence of prepared positions would

---

117. "Forward Defense of Europe," pp. 11–17. Tillson believes that the various NATO nations should maintain current active deployments in any defensive zone during peacetime and keep a few regular forces there after mobilization to augment reserve forces. This would meet de Maiziere's concern ("Rational Deployment of Forces," p. 38) that, for deterrence reasons, a defensive zone should not be manned by West Germans alone.

118. "Forward Defense of Europe," p. 5.

119. Ibid., pp. 5, 13. Tillson envisions defensive preparations occupying only 0.12 percent of a 40-by-800-kilometer zone along its eastern border, and only 0.02 percent of all West Germany.

120. Ibid., p. 5.

121. Ibid.

122. "Rational Deployment of Forces," p. 37.

enhance the credibility of NATO's claim to a defensive posture and suggests that this would facilitate its response to warning: "Fewer men and tanks would have to sprint toward the border, and this makes the change [from a peacetime] posture less arguably threatening to the East." At the same time, Betts suggests that a fortified zone could lessen the impact of surprise: "If NATO units are permitted to move out of garrisons, say, only twelve hours before Soviet tanks come over the border, they will be more effective than they would be without prefortification."[123] Even de Maiziere admits that the existence of prepared positions could lessen the threat of surprise attack.[124]

It thus appears that most observers would agree that defensive positions and prepared terrain, while by no means impregnable, could be militarily useful. Significant political objections to their creation, however, would have to be overcome. While favoring defensive preparations along the entire length of the border, Tillson feels that "initial efforts should probably be made in the most critical areas, such as the North German Plain and the Fulda Gap."[125] The limitation of a program of defensive preparations to such areas would, conceivably, be less politically troublesome and still be militarily useful.

Western Europe's willingness to undertake substantial improvements in its ground forces—even putting cost considerations aside—remains questionable. Although the allies "have increasingly come to accept the need for strong conventional forces," as Hunt notes, "they have stopped short of wanting to build up [their] role to such a point that the nuclear element would be markedly downgraded."[126] The allies' reluctance to do anything that might weaken the nuclear link between a European battlefield and the United States is well known. The foreign affairs council directors, however, in their report on Western security repeatedly mention American irritation, whether justified or not, with the continual reluctance of Western European countries to improve their defense capabilities. They note that "there is in some American circles the temptation to pressure Europe into action and, failing that, to leave

---

123. Betts, *Surprise Attack*, p. 226.
124. De Maiziere notes that defensive preparations might force an aggressor to employ stronger forces and prepare an attack more carefully, thus preventing a broad surprise attack and giving the defense time to achieve full readiness, mobilize reserve units, and bring in reinforcements. "Rational Deployment of Forces," pp. 37–38.
125. "Forward Defense of Europe," p. 17.
126. "Alternative Conventional Force Postures," p. 134.

it to its own fate."¹²⁷ Commenting on these dangers back in 1974, Michael Howard, the Oxford historian, remarked that statesmen would need time to decide and suggested that their willingness to use nuclear weapons would grow with the duration of a conflict. Hence, "a substantial conventional option does not reduce the effectiveness of nuclear deterrence: in so far as it creates the only circumstances in which the decision to use nuclear weapons becomes at all probable it considerably enhances it." He goes on to argue that "a Western Europe which could rely on its own resources to defend itself . . . would be likely to command more respect as an ally of the United States." He concludes that "American loyalty to the alliance would certainly not be weakened by a strategic reorganization based on the assumption that Western Europe intended to rely primarily upon its own efforts."¹²⁸ Theoretical objections to substantial improvements in Western Europe's defense capabilities thus are also a matter for debate.

Thinking about Military Specialization

How might all these different proposals for changing the contributions of the United States and its allies be integrated? One set of commentators would prefer greater military specialization by region, while another group would differentiate by military functions within specific regions.

Regional Specialization

Calling for greater military specialization within the West, Senator Nunn notes that "the United States possesses inherent advantages in strategic and theater nuclear arms, in naval power, and in the ability to project military force in areas distant from Europe." While claiming that "the security of Western Europe today is just as sensitive to events in the Middle East and in the Indian Ocean as it is to events along the German border," the senator points out that the countries of Western Europe, "for political as well as military reasons, are not in a position to unilaterally guarantee their own securities against nuclear threats or against threats to their economic lifeline outside of Europe." They do,

---

127. Kaiser and others, *Western Security*, pp. 12–13, 15, 18, 27.
128. Howard, "NATO and the Year of Europe," p. 27.

however, "enjoy a natural advantage in conventional ground and tactical air forces confined to the European theater," according to Nunn.[129]

This exposition of differences in comparative military advantage within NATO could logically be taken to mean, first of all, that the United States should assume sole responsibility for meeting military threats to vital Western interests outside Europe. Since constraints on its defense resources will remain, the United States would somehow decrease its contribution to NATO's central front in order to guarantee the availability of resources to preserve its nuclear capabilities and its capacity to intervene in other areas. The latter requirement would presumably involve the maintenance of four or so highly ready and fully supported divisions, prompt procurement of the strategic mobility assets needed to permit their more timely deployment to distant regions, and some expansion of U.S. naval and perhaps air forces. As their indirect contribution to seemingly more pressing requirements in the Persian Gulf (or wherever), the allies would be expected to compensate for decreases in U.S. ground capabilities vis-à-vis the central front.

Not surprisingly, Senator Nunn does not actually go this far. Nunn and most observers would probably agree with Albert Wohlstetter's view that plans for a unilateral U.S. defense of Western interests in the third world are politically unacceptable.[130] The common perception is that Americans would be unwilling to carry the security burdens outside Europe alone and that potential allies in other regions would be more willing to accept U.S. help if it was cloaked in a multinational effort. Nunn, in fact, believes that the United States should remain the leading partner outside Europe, but with some allied help. He maintains, however, that while the United States should also stay a contributing partner in Europe, "our NATO allies must become leading partners in achieving essential equivalence in the conventional arena."[131]

Functional Specialization

The Reagan administration appears to favor a four-tiered arrangement for meeting military threats in Europe and beyond.[132] The United States

129. "Defense Budget and Defense Capabilities," pp. 387–88.
130. "Meeting the Threat in the Persian Gulf," *Survey,* vol. 25 (Spring 1980), p. 167.
131. "Defense Budget and Defense Capabilities," pp. 388–89.
132. See Frank C. Carlucci, remarks delivered at the 18th annual Wehrkunde Conference, Munich, February 21, 1981.

would bear most of the responsibility for any contingency outside Europe. Token force contributions, however, would be provided by certain allies, presumably such as France and Britain. More important, the countries of Western Europe would fill in at home for U.S. forces diverted from NATO. Finally, to provide encouragement and some compensation, the United States would make modest additional contributions toward central Europe.

How might additional efforts in Europe be divided up among the United States and the allies? Most observers would agree with Nunn that Western Europe enjoys inherent advantages in its ability to deploy ground forces on the central front. At the same time, some would argue that it would be easier for the United States to deploy additional naval and air rather than ground forces to Europe. Canby, for one, feels that the United States should offer to assume more of the responsibility for meeting NATO air and naval requirements in return for greater ground force contributions from the allies. He believes that if allied air and naval budgets were reduced 30 percent, the allies could organize enough reserve units to triple their total division count at no additional cost. The reduction in their air assets "could be replaced at virtually no cost by the United States, resulting in no loss in overall air capability."[133] Although the basis for these claims and the practicability of a program of this magnitude would no doubt be questioned, many analysts would probably accept the logic underlying Canby's proposal. Most observers also believe that the United States should continue planning for NATO's reinforcement. Increased allied ground contributions, however, might well allow the United States to plan on more deliberate reinforcement. This would alleviate the doubts some have about the wisdom of current plans for rapid reinforcement and would perhaps permit greater U.S. reliance on reserve forces, a step that some think might help ease the problems of a tight supply of manpower.

Proposals for such military specialization and collectively balanced forces date back to the early days of NATO. Observers have always admitted that they make some sense. General de Maiziere notes that specialization along service lines "would open vast possibilities for rationalisation. Logistics and training could be considerably reduced and become less expensive." He, however, raises the usual objection to

133. Canby, *Short (And Long) War Responses,* pp. 95–98. Canby notes that several factors, such as the availability of airfields, would constrain U.S. air deployments to Europe.

such proposals: "For some partners the system would result in a high degree of dependence on the solidarity of the Alliance."[134] Sloss makes the same objection and adds that "the prospect of fierce inter-service rivalries over what is to be relinquished" is a major obstacle.[135] No one, however, denies the fact that NATO countries are already highly dependent on each other for their security. In any case, advocates of greater military specialization such as Canby are not suggesting, for instance, that the countries of Western Europe completely scrap their navies and air forces for the sake of ground force improvements.[136] Sloss also worries that specialization "could simply become a rationale for doing less."[137] It was the early 1970s, however, when Sloss and de Maiziere raised these objections to specialization. Nunn and others believe that developments since then in central Europe and elsewhere warrant fresh consideration of some form of greater military specialization among Western nations.

134. "Rational Deployment of Forces," p. 46.
135. *NATO Reform*, p. 55.
136. The cuts Canby speaks of—30 percent—should, for instance, at least permit Western European countries to retain aircraft for air defense and ships for minesweeping and coastal defense.
137. *NATO Reform*, p. 55.

CHAPTER FIVE

CONCLUSIONS

EUROPEAN requirements will, by all expectations, continue to drive U.S. ground force planning. This is understandable. Although its chances are remote, the outbreak of another European war would be an enormous disaster. The United States clearly has a vital interest in helping preserve the territorial and political integrity of Western Europe. Most observers would agree that, in an age of nuclear plenty, conventional forces must be the primary means for deterring conventional aggression.

The military situation in central Europe offers some basis for assurance, at least when reasonable standards are applied and reasonable assumptions made. Admittedly, NATO cannot derive high confidence from the quantitative balance of ground forces; but neither should the West feel pessimistic about its defensive prospects. Projections based on a range of expert opinion about the military potential of both NATO and Warsaw Pact forces indicate that neither side could count on achieving a decisive numerical edge. Under these circumstances, the outcome of a conflict could well hinge on factors other than numbers of troops and weapons. In some areas, such as air power, NATO seems to enjoy advantages that could compensate for numerical shortcomings in ground combat power.

Specific judgments on the adequacy of NATO's ground forces depend on the strategic perspective from which these forces are viewed. When the central front is considered in isolation, a compelling need for additional NATO ground forces does not emerge. While extra forces could provide greater confidence, it has been shown that the numerical balance already lies within a tolerable range. One might, in the absence of further study, just as well argue that NATO could most efficiently gain leverage by pursuing improvements in such things as readiness, command and control, logistics, and air power. When central Europe is placed in a global context, however, it is easier to argue that NATO should expand its forces, mainly to allow for a possible diversion of U.S. reinforcements to one or more contingencies outside Europe. Limited wars in Korea and Southeast Asia have made substantial demands on the strategic reserve of U.S. ground forces in the past. More recently, developments in Southwest Asia have added potential demands not allowed for by the current U.S. force structure. Those taking a sanguine view of the likelihood of multiple contingencies and of potential links between European and other conflicts, however, might still dismiss any need for additional ground forces.

If NATO does elect to create more ground forces, military logic would hold that they should be provided by the countries of Western Europe. Experts agree that Western Europe has the potential to mobilize and deploy ground forces to the central front more rapidly than could the United States. Among the various options for strengthening Western European armies that have been suggested, the strongest case has been made for creating additional reserve combat units. Supporters have pointed out that reserve combat forces, exploiting forested or built-up terrain, could serve as a valuable supplement to high-quality regular forces. The construction of fortifications in vulnerable border areas could raise the military effectiveness of reserve combatants. It has been suggested that this combination of selective fortification and additional reserve combat units would improve NATO's capacity for meeting a short-warning attack. The personnel for additional reserve forces could come from the large number of trained soldiers—most of whom are now assigned to individual reserve replacement pools—that the conscript armies of the continental countries turn out every year. Indications are that the cost of equipping reservists as antitank infantry and of building fortifications in selected areas need not be high. The countries of Western Europe are reluctant, however, to increase the amount they spend on defense.

A solution to this problem may lie in proposals for a functional division of military effort. It is easier for the United States to project air and naval forces than ground forces, as shown in past wars (World War II and Korea) and as recognized in NATO's original defense plan (January 1950). There are again proposals that the United States should offer to assume more of the NATO naval and air burden. The intent would be to free Western European resources for such things as equipping new reserve combat units. This old idea deserves fresh attention.

Conclusions 103

As for U.S. ground forces themselves, a convincing case for substantial changes in deployments or force structure has not been made. A reduction in the American ground contribution to NATO—whether out of pique or pessimism—would generally be thought an inappropriate and imprudent move that would erode what confidence NATO can now feel about its defensive prospects and politically unsettle the Western Europeans, who would not necessarily move to take up the slack. At the other extreme, an increase in the U.S. ground contribution seems unwarranted and unlikely. Reasonable assessments should indicate that the military balance in central Europe is not precarious. Moreover, many observers would argue that military threats to Western security are more likely to arise elsewhere in the world and that the United States should first attend to military needs outside Europe.

But some redirection of the U.S. ground contribution to NATO may be appropriate in light of strong arguments for a shift in emphasis from rapid to deliberate reinforcement. This would involve, first, greater reliance on ships for movement of forces. Serious questions have been raised about the security and reliability of the prepositioning of equipment and airlift of troops that current plans are based on. Moreover, there is justifiable concern that extensive prepositioning on the continent locks much of the United States' strategic ground reserve into NATO and leaves it less ready to meet limited contingencies outside Europe. In contrast, moving troops by sea is credited with offering advantages in efficiency, reliability, and flexibility. The greater strategic mobility that would result from increased availability of sealift could also provide an impetus for a program to raise the readiness of the reserve components. The reserves would benefit from larger procurement and training budgets and perhaps from such organizational innovations that have been suggested as the assignment of some regular personnel to serve as active cadres. An ability by the United States to deploy a larger number of readier reserve units more rapidly would brighten NATO's defensive prospects; for analysis here of the quantitative ground balance indicates that any NATO shortfalls are more likely to develop several weeks after the start of mobilization. It would be unfair, since the reserves suffered from serious personnel and equipment shortages, to use problems in past mobilizations as an excuse for avoiding reserve component improvements.

More generally, there needs to be more explicit consideration of the trade-offs in its ground posture that the United States might make between requirements for deterring a general war in Europe and those for deterring or prosecuting limited wars, the latter of which seem more likely to occur. For instance, it may be that the reserve components should focus only on Europe and not be counted on to contribute to U.S. capabilities for limited war. If this is so, it also may be that the active forces, which are responsible for a contingency anywhere, are too dependent on the reserve components for logistical support. Whatever the case, while regional military balances and strategic considerations are important, there is a wealth of historical experience that should also be drawn upon to help answer important questions about the future shape of U.S. ground forces.

APPENDIX A

Estimating Ground Combat Potential

ANY NUMBER of static indicators can be used to compare the combat potential of ground forces. These include numbers of divisions, total ground manpower, manpower in major combat (divisional or brigade-sized) units, weapons counts, and such indexes as armored division equivalents.

No single static indicator is wholly satisfactory, but some are regarded as more useful than others.[1] Simple division counts are criticized on the grounds that the divisions of different armies—even if of the same type—normally differ in size, organization, and combat potential.[2] Lucas Fischer, of the Arms Control and Disarmament Agency, maintains that total manpower is not a particularly useful measure because different countries count ground personnel differently and allocate them differently between combat and support roles. He argues that the "ratio of men in major combat units would seem the best single indicator of immediate ground combat capability"; he grants, however, that strength of other combat units, weapons density, and weapons quality should also be considered.[3]

Comparative counts of tanks, missiles, artillery, and so forth have been criticized for ignoring the potential interactions among different

1. This discussion draws, in part, on Congressional Budget Office (CBO), *Assessing the NATO/Warsaw Pact Military Balance,* prepared by James Blaker and Andrew Hamilton (U.S. Government Printing Office, 1977), pp. 53–61.
2. For examples of differences in divisional organization, see International Institute for Strategic Studies, *The Military Balance, 1977–1978* (London: IISS, 1977), pp. 92–93; *1978–1979,* pp. 101–03; *1980–1981,* pp. vii, 98–101.
3. Robert Lucas Fischer, *Defending the Central Front: The Balance of Forces,* Adelphi Paper 127 (London: IISS, 1976), pp. 7, 15. Manpower in major combat units has served as an indicator in other assessments as well. For example, see CBO, *Strengthening NATO: Pomcus and Other Approaches,* prepared by Pat Hillier (CBO, 1979), p. 54.

categories of weapons. This shortcoming has inspired the development of indexing methods that reduce opposing forces to a common basis for comparison. One method takes into account the firepower, mobility, and survivability of its individual weapons to produce for any given unit a weighted unit value (WUV), which can alternatively be expressed in terms of armored division equivalents (ADEs). Although WUV/ADE counts "ideally represent actual combat experience filtered through the perceptions of military men," two analysts in the Congressional Budget Office note that this methodology "necessarily introduces great subjectivity to the weighting process."[4] Defense Department analysts note that since war reserve stocks are not counted, armies that practice individual rather than unit replacement are penalized, but they feel this methodology provides a much better basis for assessment than "bean counts" of divisions or weapons.[5] This appendix estimates the strength of NATO and Warsaw Pact forces in terms of both manpower in major combat units and armored division equivalents.

Manpower in Major Combat Units

The calculation here of the number of men in major combat units reflects average, wartime personnel strengths. The figures are merely approximations, since military organization is flexible and subunits may be added or detached. Moreover, during peacetime, units may be manned at substantially lower levels than an organization chart indicates.

NATO Forces

The armies of NATO contain a variety of units of varying sizes. Table A-1 lists the standard personnel strengths of units for which figures are available. The tables compiled by the International Institute for Strategic Studies (IISS) imply that the totals for Belgian, Dutch, and Danish

---

4. CBO, *Assessing the NATO/Warsaw Pact Military Balance*, p. 57.
5. Practically all the equipment in Warsaw Pact armies is assigned to units, which would be replaced after their depletion in combat by fresh units. The U.S. Army emphasizes the replacement of combat losses on an individual basis; the substantial amounts of equipment it maintains in war reserve stockpiles to that end are not counted in ADE tallies.

divisions would be similar to those for West German divisions.[6] In this study it is assumed that 4,000 men each would be found in Dutch infantry brigades and British field forces (motorized infantry brigades), and 3,000 men each in West Germany's home defense regiments.

Warsaw Pact Forces

The organization of Warsaw Pact divisions is less standardized than is commonly supposed. The IISS suggests personnel complements of 11,000 men in Warsaw Pact armored divisions and 14,000 in mechanized divisions.[7] A European expert, however, cites ranges of 9,450–11,000 for Soviet armored divisions and 11,500–13,150 for Soviet mechanized divisions and maintains that Eastern European divisions tend to be smaller than their Soviet counterparts.[8]

This study assumes that, in almost all cases, armored divisions would comprise 11,000 men, mechanized divisions 13,000 men, and airborne divisions 7,000 men. Divisions of the Group of Soviet Forces in Germany (GSFG) appear to be larger than the norm, however. Reports that GSFG armored divisions are receiving three full battalions of additional infantry and three additional artillery battalions, and that each already has 90 extra tanks, point to an average personnel strength of 13,200. The reported assignment of an additional artillery battalion to GSFG mechanized divisions suggests a personnel strength of 13,300.[9] Apparent shortages of equipment among many divisions stationed in the Soviet interior suggest that their personnel strengths are below those assumed here; in this study, however, it is assumed that any divisions from the Soviet interior assigned to take part in an attack in central Europe would be full-sized. The Czechoslovak airborne regiment is assumed to contain 2,000 men.

---

6. IISS, *Military Balance, 1981–1982*, p. vii.
7. Ibid.
8. Friedrich Wiener, *The Armies of the Warsaw Pact Nations*, 3d ed. (Vienna: Carl Ueberreuter, 1981), pp. 68–70.
9. The reports include Richard Burt, *New York Times*, June 8, 1980; "Soviet Divisions Receive Extra Artillery and Infantry," *International Defense Review*, vol. 13, no. 6 (1980), p. 802. Estimated strengths are based on these two sources and U.S. Department of the Army, *Handbook on Soviet Ground Forces*, FM30-40 (GPO, 1976), app. A.

Armored Division Equivalents

Since 1971, armored division equivalents (ADEs) have been used in official U.S. studies to assess the strength of ground forces.[10] The estimates of force strengths are based on standard measures of weapon effectiveness developed by the U.S. Army. Each weapon is rated against the standard for its category, which produces a weapon effectiveness index (WEI). For example, the Soviet T62 tank when measured against that category's standard—a U.S. M60A1 tank (1.0)—has a WEI of 1.03.[11] Each of the weapon categories is assigned a weight—the tanks weapon category, for instance, has been assigned an average weight of 60, in contrast to 1.1 for small arms. The WEIs of all the weapons in each category of any given unit are added together and their sum multiplied by the category weight; the weighted sums of all categories are then added together to produce a weighted unit value (WUV) for that unit. Thus, the average WUV of a U.S. armored division is 48,586 and of a Soviet armored division 31,856.[12] With the WUV of a U.S. armored division providing the standard for comparison, a U.S. armored division is defined as being worth 1.0 ADE, while its Soviet counterpart is worth 0.66 ADE.

The ADE figures presented here are derived from the Army's 1974 compilation of weapon effectiveness indexes and weighted unit values and from tables of organization and equipment that are publicly available. While the indexes and weights now used by the Army may be somewhat different, those developed for the 1974 manual should have been reasonably sound. The 1974 values would probably produce substantially the same results as later indexes and weights.

The estimates presented here may not coincide with official ADE scores, however, since equipment counts may differ. The weapons

---

10. Another method, popular before the 1970s, drew on ballistic research on lethal area and tank-kill probability and would assign a firepower score to any given weapon. The scores of every weapon in any given unit were then added together to produce an overall firepower score for that unit. See U.S. Department of the Army, *Maneuver Control*, FM105-5 (1973), apps. E, F, G. This method was criticized for being arbitrary and poorly supported by theory or combat experience, and for being influenced by the subjective interpretation of laboratory data.

11. U.S. Army, Concepts Analysis Agency, *Weapon Effectiveness Indices/Weighted Unit Values (WEI/WUV)* (1974), vol. 1, p. 26.

12. Ibid.

counted here exclude attack helicopters and antiaircraft artillery, on the grounds that the former have more in common with aircraft and that aircraft are the principal target of the latter. Nor are bazooka-type antitank rockets counted since figures are not available for all units. The most reliable means for estimating the number of small arms in a unit was to multiply the number of infantry units (usually battalions) within a larger formation by the number of armored personnel carriers in each infantry unit and multiply that product by the number of infantrymen in each carrier.

While it is most unlikely that the weighted unit values derived here would correspond with those produced within the Defense Department, the ADE scores for given units would probably be reasonably close. The tables in this appendix illustrate the derivation of WUV and ADE scores for major NATO and Warsaw Pact units.[13]

NATO Forces

By definition, a standard U.S. armored division (table A-2) is worth 1.0 ADE. It is assumed here that U.S. armored divisions based in Europe are worth 1.07 ADEs, however, because they are assigned extra artillery and armored reconnaissance vehicles and have been receiving M60A3 tanks and improved TOW vehicles. Likewise, U.S. mechanized divisions based in Europe are assumed to be worth 1.01 ADEs, in contrast to the 0.94 ADE for the standard division (table A-3). The U.S. Army's 1974 values are 0.87 ADE for its infantry divisions, 0.69 ADE for its airborne divisions, and 0.77 ADE for its air-mobile divisions. It is assumed here that the weapons contents would amount to 0.30 ADE for an armored brigade, 0.28 ADE for a mechanized brigade, and 0.25 ADE for an infantry brigade. An armored cavalry regiment, usually assigned to a corps, possesses a rating of 0.39 ADE. The artillery units attached to a U.S. corps would, as table A-4 indicates, contribute about 0.17 ADE worth of combat potential.[14] This study assumes that their possession of

---

13. Although other studies have presented ADE counts and ratios, their lack of explicitness about the underlying assumptions should raise questions about the conclusions of the analysis. For example, see CBO, *U.S. Ground Forces: Design and Cost Alternatives for NATO and Non-NATO Contingencies,* prepared by Pat Hillier and Nora Slatkin (CBO, 1980), pp. 22–25.

14. Estimated ADEs are based on U.S. Army, *Weapon Effectiveness Indices/ Weighted Unit Values,* pp. 26–28, 35, 42, 44; *Department of Defense Annual Report,*

older equipment would lower the ADE value of reserve component units, except for round-out brigades, to 96 percent that of their active U.S.-based counterparts.

Each of West Germany's armored divisions would have a rating of 0.72 ADE and each of its mechanized divisions 0.71 ADE (tables A-5 and A-6). The artillery units in a West German corps would, as table A-4 shows, contribute another 0.05 ADE worth of combat potential. The Belgian, Dutch, and Danish counterparts that the IISS suggests are organized along similar lines would have the same ADE ratings as the West German units. An airborne brigade, worth perhaps 0.13 ADE, would also be assigned to each West German corps. As for the combat units in West Germany's Territorial Army, it is assumed that contributions would amount to 0.21 ADE for each home defense brigade, 0.11 ADE for each heavy home defense regiment, and 0.04 ADE for each light home defense regiment.[15]

British forces are less heavily equipped. A British armored division would weigh in at only 0.49 ADE (table A-7) and the modest artillery assets assigned to the British corps would contribute a mere 0.01 ADE worth of combat power. The corps would, however, also control one or more field forces. Each of these brigade-sized formations of motorized infantry contains weapons worth about 0.19 ADE. This study assumes the same value for the infantry brigade in the Dutch reserves.[16]

The French Army in 1978 doubled its number of maneuver divisions, essentially by splitting the old division in two. As tables A-8 and A-9 indicate, a French armored division would contribute about 0.30 worth of weaponry while a French mechanized division would add about 0.24 ADE. The value of combat and combat-support assets in a French corps

---

Fiscal Year 1982, pp. 134–37; IISS, *Military Balance, 1977–1978*, pp. 92–93; Charles Kamps, Jr., "The Next War: Modern Conflict in Europe," *Strategy and Tactics*, no. 69 (July–August 1978), p. 31.

15. Estimated ADEs are based on West German Minister of Defense, *White Paper 1979: The Security of the Federal Republic of Germany and the Development of the Federal Armed Forces* (Federal Minister of Defense, 1979), pp. 152–56; information provided by the Washington embassy of the Federal Republic of Germany; Otto von Pivka, *The Armies of Europe Today* (Reading, England: Osprey, 1974); Kamps, "The Next War," p. 33; U.S. Army, *Weapon Effectiveness Indices/Weighted Unit Values*, pp. 24, 26, 28–29, 31, 38, 42.

16. Estimated ADEs are based on Lt. Gen. Sir William Scotter, "The British Army Today," *Journal of the Royal United Services Institute for Defence Studies*, vol. 121 (June 1976), p. 18; Kamps, "The Next War," p. 32; U.S. Army, *Weapon Effectiveness Indices/Weighted Unit Values*, pp. 24, 26, 28–29, 31, 38, 42.

amounts, as table A-4 indicates, to 0.16 ADE. Canada's mechanized brigade group is assumed to possess another 0.22 ADE worth of combat potential.[17]

Warsaw Pact Forces

Soviet divisions, even those of the same type, vary in regard to the quantity and quality of their equipment. Tables A-10 and A-11 portray the value of the equipment likely to be found in armored and mechanized divisions based in the western military districts of the Soviet Union. They receive ratings of 0.66 and 0.68 ADE. The WEI assigned to their tanks is an average for the tank inventory found in western Russia.[18] Soviet divisions based in Eastern Europe tend to be larger. Forward-deployed mechanized divisions apparently have been assigned an extra tank battalion. This would raise the value of Soviet mechanized divisions in the Central Group of Forces (CGF) to 0.73 ADE. Divisions in the Group of Soviet Forces in Germany (GSFG) have been strengthened still further and have received more new equipment. The presence of additional infantrymen, tanks, armored fighting vehicles, artillery, antitank weapons, and mortars in GSFG armored divisions raises the value of each to 0.90 ADE. Likewise, a GSFG mechanized division is worth 0.76 ADE. Although there is evidence (see chapter 3) of equipment shortfalls for some lower-readiness forces, this study assumes that all divisions that might come from the Soviet interior would be fully equipped. Their possession of older equipment would, however, lower values to 0.63 ADE for an armored division and 0.64 ADE for a mechanized division. A Soviet airborne division is assumed to be worth 0.24 ADE.[19]

---

17. Estimated ADEs are based on IISS, *Military Balance, 1980–1981*, p. 23; U.S. Army, *Weapon Effectiveness Indices/Weighted Unit Values*, pp. 24, 26, 28–29, 31, 38, 42.

18. Varying mixes of T54, T55, T62, T64, and T72 tanks are found with Soviet forces in Eastern Europe and throughout the Soviet Union. For a breakdown of the inventories held by different groups or in different districts, see *International Defense Review*, vol. 13, no. 1 (1980), pp. 20–22. The WEIs for T54s, T55s, and T62s are found in U.S. Army, *Weapon Effectiveness Indices/Weighted Unit Values*, p. 26. The WEI for T64s and T72s is assumed to be 1.17, equivalent to that for a Leopard-2 armed with a 120 mm gun. Based on the mix of tanks, average tank WEIs are 1.06 for the GSFG; 1.02 for other Soviet forces in Eastern Europe or in the Leningrad, Baltic, Belorussian, or Carpathian districts; and 0.97 for Soviet forces based elsewhere.

19. Estimated ADEs are based on IISS, *Military Balance, 1978–1979*, pp. 102–03; U.S. Department of the Army, *Handbook on Soviet Ground Forces*, app. A; C. N.

Although organized along Soviet lines, the divisions of Eastern European countries vary somewhat, even among themselves. They tend to have less tube artillery and more multiple rocket launchers than Soviet divisions.[20] Some of the armies' inventories of armored fighting vehicles include many locally produced items (for example, the OT65 armored personnel carrier), while the equipment in others is almost entirely Soviet-designed. The T55 is still the mainstay of Eastern European tank units, with the arrival of some T72s assumed to be offset for the time being by the presence of yet older T54s. Tables A-12 and A-13 thus represent only what might be considered typical Eastern European divisions. Weapon contents amount to 0.59 ADE for an Eastern European armored division and 0.65 ADE for a mechanized division. This study assumes values of 0.24 ADE for the Polish airborne division and 0.07 ADE for the Czech airborne regiment.

Finally, some proportion of the Warsaw Pact's combat potential would reside in units held at the army or front level. Table A-14 derives ADE values for three such units.

Donnelly, "Operations in the Enemy Rear: Soviet Doctrine and Tactics," *International Defense Review*, vol. 13, no. 1 (1980), p. 36; U.S. Army, *Weapon Effectiveness Indices/Weighted Unit Values*, pp. 25–27, 29–30, 32–34, 39, 42.

20. See IISS, *Military Balance, 1978–1979*, pp. 102–03; *1980–1981*, pp. 15–17.

Table A-1. Personnel Strengths for Selected NATO Units

Country and type of unit	Number of men in Division	Number of men in Brigade or regiment
Canada		
Mechanized	...	3,000
France		
Armored	7,000	...
Mechanized	6,900	...
Great Britain		
Armored	11,500	...
United States		
Armored	18,900	4,500
Mechanized	18,500	4,800
Infantry	18,100	4,000
Airborne	16,700	...
Air mobile	18,300	...
Armored cavalry	...	3,200
West Germany[a]		
Armored	17,000	...
Mechanized	17,500	3,700
Airborne	...	2,300

Sources: International Institute for Strategic Studies, *The Military Balance, 1980–1981* (London: IISS, 1980), pp. vii, 6, 23, 98, 99; Thomas A. Dine and others, "The Defense Budget," in Joseph A. Pechman, ed., *Setting National Priorities: The 1980 Budget* (Brookings Institution, 1979), p. 197; U.S. Department of the Army, *Staff Officers' Field Manual: Organizational Technical and Logistic Data*, FM101-10-1 (Department of the Army, 1976), p. 2/117; Charles Kamps, Jr., "The Next War: Modern Conflict in Europe," *Strategy and Tactics*, no. 69 (July–August 1978), p. 33.

a. Most West German brigades would be incorporated into divisions. But the Territorial Army contains separate mechanized brigades, while airborne forces would apparently operate as brigades.

Table A-2. Relative Value of Equipment in a U.S. Armored Division

Weapon category	Number of weapons	×	Weapon effectiveness index	×	Category weight (defensive)	=	Weighted value
Small arms	2,880[a]		1.00		1.2		3,456
Armored personnel carriers							
M113A1	376		1.00		6.0		2,256
M114A1	179		0.93		6.0		999
Tanks							
M60A1	324		1.00		55.0		17,820
Armored reconnaissance vehicles							
M551	27		1.00		36.0		972
Antitank weapons							
TOW/M113A1	90		1.00		46.0		4,140
Dragon	254		0.64		46.0		7,478
Artillery							
M109A1	54		1.00[b]		85.0		4,590
M110A1	12		1.15[b]		85.0		1,173
Mortars							
M106A1	53		1.00		47.0		2,491
M125A1	45		1.00		47.0		2,115
Weighted unit value	. . .		. . .		. . .		47,490
Armored division equivalent	. . .		. . .		. . .		1.00

Sources: IISS, *Military Balance, 1978–1979*, p. 101; U.S. Army, Concepts Analysis Agency, *Weapon Effectiveness Indices/Weighted Unit Values (WEI/WUV)* (1974), vol. 1, pp. 24, 26–28, 35, 38, 42.

a. Based on a division with 5 mechanized battalions, each with 48 M113A1 personnel carriers, each of which carries 12 infantrymen.

b. Firing improved conventional munitions.

Table A-3. Relative Value of Equipment in a U.S. Mechanized Division

Weapon category	Number of weapons	×	Weapon effectiveness index	×	Category weight (defensive)	=	Weighted value
Small arms	3,456[a]		1.00		1.2		4,147
Armored personnel carriers							
M113A1	406		1.00		6.0		2,436
M114A1	176		0.93		6.0		982
Tanks							
M60A1	216		1.00		55.0		11,880
Armored reconnaissance vehicles							
M551	27		1.00		36.0		972
Antitank weapons							
TOW/M113A1	108		1.00		46.0		4,968
Dragon	294		0.64		46.0		8,655
Artillery							
M109A1	54		1.00[b]		85.0		4,590
M110A1	12		1.15[b]		85.0		1,173
Mortars							
M106A1	49		1.00		47.0		2,303
M125A1	54		1.00		47.0		2,538
Weighted unit value	...		...		...		44,644
Armored division equivalent	...		...		...		0.94

Sources: IISS, *Military Balance, 1978–1979*, p. 101; U.S. Army, *Weapon Effectiveness Indices/Weighted Unit Values*, vol. 1, pp. 24, 26–28, 35, 38, 42.

a. Based on a division with 6 mechanized battalions, each with 48 M113A1 personnel carriers, each of which carries 12 infantrymen.

b. Firing improved conventional munitions.

Table A-4. Relative Value of Equipment in Units Attached to NATO Corps

Formation and weapon category	Number of weapons	×	Weapon effectiveness index	×	Category weight (defensive)	=	Weighted value
British Corps[a]							
Artillery							
M110A1	16		0.52		85.0		707
WUV	...		...		...		707
ADE	...		...		...		0.01
French Corps							
Artillery							
AMX-GCT	30		0.60[b]		85.0		1,530
Small arms	950		1.00[c,d]		1.2		1,140
Armored personnel carriers							
VAB	95		0.85[c,e]		6.0		485
Antitank weapons							
Milan	24		0.65[c]		46.0		718
Mortars							
AMX/81	8		0.98[c]		47.0		368
AMX/120	42		1.11[c,f]		47.0		2,191
Armored reconnaissance vehicles							
AML/90	36		0.64[f]		36.0		829
WUV	...		...		...		7,261
ADE	...		...		...		0.15
U.S. Corps[g]							
Artillery							
M107	24		0.46		85.0		938
M110A1	72		1.15[h]		85.0		7,038
WUV	...		...		...		7,976
ADE	...		...		...		0.17
West German Corps[i]							
Artillery							
FH70	18		0.49[b]		85.0		750
M101A1	36		0.49[j]		85.0		1,449
WUV	...		...		...		2,249
ADE	...		...		...		0.05

Sources: Phillip A. Karber, *Force Restructuring and New Weapons Technologies: Relationships in NATO Armies & Operations* (McLean, Va.: BDM Corp., 1978), pp. 34, 39, 45, 50; Gerard Turbe, "The French Army of the Eighties," *Armies & Weapons*, 1977, p. 23; IISS, *Military Balance, 1980–1981*, pp. 21, 99; U.S. Army, *Weapon Effectiveness Indices/Weighted Unit Values*, vol. 1, pp. 27–28, 31–32, 34–35, 38, 42.

WUV Weighted unit value.
ADE Armored division equivalent.
a. Excludes infantry field forces (brigades).
b. Firing 95 percent high-explosive projectiles and 5 percent high-explosive, rocket-assisted projectiles.
c. With motor infantry regiment attached to corps.
d. Assumes 95 VAB personnel carriers with 10 infantrymen each.
e. Estimate.
f. With 2 reconnaissance regiments attached to corps.
g. Excludes maneuver brigades or regiments.
h. Firing improved conventional munitions.
i. Excludes airborne brigade.
j. Firing high-explosive, high-fragmentation projectiles.

Table A-5. Relative Value of Equipment in a West German Armored Division

Weapon category	Number of weapons	×	Weapon effectiveness index	×	Category weight (defensive)	=	Weighted value
Small arms	2,284[a]		1.00		1.2		2,741
Armored personnel carriers							
Marder	250		1.25		6.0		1,875
Tanks							
Leopard-1	300		1.06		55.0		17,490
Antitank weapons							
JPzK/90	16		0.53		46.0		390
JPzR/TOW	34		1.10[b]		46.0		1,720
Milan	152		0.65		46.0		4,545
Artillery							
M109A1	54		0.62[c]		85.0		2,846
M107	12		0.46		85.0		469
M110A1	6		0.52		85.0		265
LARS	16		0.47		85.0		639
Mortars							
M113/120	24		1.13		47.0		1,275
Weighted unit value	...		...		...		34,255
Armored division equivalent	...		...		...		0.72

Sources: Karber, *Force Restructuring and New Weapons Technologies*, p. 39; West German Minister of Defense, *White Paper 1979: The Security of the Federal Republic of Germany and the Development of the Federal Armed Forces* (Minister of Defense, 1979), p. 153; Otto von Pivka, *The Armies of Europe Today* (Reading, England: Osprey, 1974); U.S. Army, *Weapon Effectiveness Indices/Weighted Unit Values*, vol. 1, pp. 24, 26, 28–29, 31, 34, 38, 42.

a. Assumes 7 infantrymen in each of 184 Marder personnel carriers in infantry units, and 6 Jaeger companies with 166 men each.

b. Estimate.

c. Firing 95 percent high-explosive, high-fragmentation projectiles and 5 percent high-explosive, rocket-assisted projectiles.

Table A-6. **Relative Value of Equipment in a West German Mechanized Division**

Weapon category	Number of weapons	×	Weapon effectiveness index	×	Category weight (defensive)	=	Weighted value
Small arms	2,606[a]		1.00		1.2		3,127
Armored personnel carriers							
Marder	287		1.25		6.0		2,153
Tanks							
Leopard-1	250		1.06		55.0		14,575
Antitank weapons							
JPzK/90	16		0.53		46.0		390
JPzR/TOW	34		1.10[b]		46.0		1,720
Milan	193		0.65		46.0		5,771
Artillery							
M109A1	54		0.62[c]		85.0		2,846
M107	12		0.46		85.0		469
M110A1	6		0.52		85.0		265
LARS	16		0.47		85.0		639
Mortars							
M113/120	30		1.13		47.0		1,593
Weighted unit value	...		...		...		33,548
Armored division equivalent	...		...		...		0.71

Sources: Same as for table A-5.

a. Assumes 7 infantrymen in each of 230 Marder personnel carriers in infantry units, and 6 Jaeger companies with 166 men each.

b. Estimate.

c. Firing 95 percent high-explosive, high-fragmentation projectiles and 5 percent high-explosive, rocket-assisted projectiles.

Table A-7. **Relative Value of Equipment in a British Armored Division**

Weapon category	Number of weapons	×	Weapon effective- ness index	×	Category weight (defensive)	=	Weighted value
Small arms	2,340[a]		1.00		1.2		2,808
Armored personnel carriers							
FV432	325		0.78		6.0		1,521
Fox	37		0.97		6.0		215
Tanks							
Chieftain	148		1.14		55.0		9,280
Armored reconnaissance vehicles							
Scorpion	72		0.88		36.0		2,281
Antitank weapons							
FV438/Swingfire	30		0.90[b]		46.0		1,242
Milan	108		0.65		46.0		3,229
Artillery							
M107	4		0.46		85.0		156
M109A1	12		0.62[c]		85.0		632
Abbot	24		0.44		85.0		898
Mortars							
FV432/81	18		0.98		47.0		829
Weighted unit value	...		...		...		23,091
Armored division equivalent	...		...		...		0.49

Sources: Karber, *Force Restructuring and New Weapons Technologies*, p. 47; IISS, *Military Balance, 1980–1981*, p. 21; U.S. Army, *Weapon Effectiveness Indices/Weighted Unit Values*, vol. 1, pp. 24–28, 31–32, 38, 42; Kamps, "The Next War," p. 32.

a. Assumes 10 infantrymen in each of 234 FV432 personnel carriers with infantry battalions.
b. Estimate.
c. Firing 95 percent high-explosive, high-fragmentation projectiles and 5 percent high-explosive, rocket-assisted projectiles.

Table A-8. Relative Value of Equipment in a French Armored Division

Weapon category	Number of weapons	×	Weapon effectiveness index	×	Category weight (defensive)	=	Weighted value
Small arms	1,260[a]		1.00		1.2		1,512
Armored personnel carriers							
AMX-10P	142		1.23		6.0		1,048
VAB	103		0.85[b]		6.0		525
Tanks							
AMX-30	148		0.93		55.0		7,570
Antitank weapons							
VAB/HOT	12		0.70[b]		46.0		386
Milan	38		0.65		46.0		1,136
Artillery							
AMX-GCT	24		0.60[c]		85.0		1,224
Mortars							
AMX/120	12		1.11		47.0		626
Weighted unit value	...		...		...		14,027
Armored division equivalent	...		...		...		0.30

Sources: IISS, *Military Balance, 1980–1981*, pp. 98–99; U.S. Army, *Weapon Effectiveness Indices/Weighted Unit Values*, vol. 1, pp. 24, 26, 28, 32, 38, 42.
a. Based on 126 AMX-10P personnel carriers in infantry squadrons or companies, with 10 men each.
b. Estimate.
c. Firing 95 percent high-explosive projectiles and 5 percent high-explosive, rocket-assisted projectiles.

Table A-9. Relative Value of Equipment in a French Mechanized Division

Weapon category	Number of weapons	×	Weapon effectiveness index	×	Category weight (defensive)	=	Weighted value
Small arms	2,850[a]		1.00		1.2		3,420
Armored personnel carriers							
AMX-10RC	36		1.23		6.0		266
VAB	370		0.85[b]		6.0		1,887
Antitank weapons							
VAB/HOT	12		0.70[b]		46.0		386
Milan	72		0.65		46.0		2,153
Artillery							
AMX-GCT	24		0.60[c]		85.0		1,224
Mortars							
AMX/81	24		0.98		47.0		1,105
AMX/120	18		1.11		47.0		939
Weighted unit value	...		...		...		11,380
Armored division equivalent	...		...		...		0.24

Sources: Same as for table A-8.
a. Based on 285 VAB personnel carriers in infantry regiments, with 10 men each.
b. Estimate.
c. Firing 95 percent high-explosive projectiles and 5 percent high-explosive, rocket-assisted projectiles.

Table A-10. Relative Value of Equipment in a Soviet Armored Division

Weapon category	Number of weapons	×	Weapon effectiveness index	×	Category weight (offensive)	=	Weighted value
Small arms	1,116[a]		1.00		1		1,116
Armored personnel carriers							
BRDM-2	124		0.89		13		1,435
Tanks	325		1.02[b]		64		21,216
Armored reconnaissance vehicles							
PT76	22		0.75		36		594
BRDM/Sagger	9		0.70		36		227
Antitank weapons							
BMP	132		0.89		27		3,172
Sagger	12		0.50		27		162
SPG9	9		0.21		27		51
Artillery							
M1975	18		0.44[c]		72		570
M1974	6		0.44[c]		72		190
D30	36		0.40		72		1,037
BM21	18		0.54		72		700
Mortars							
M1943	18		1.01		37		673
Weighted unit value	...		...		...		31,143
Armored division equivalent	...		...		...		0.66

Sources: IISS, *Military Balance, 1978–1979*, p. 102; U.S. Army, *Weapon Effectiveness Indices/Weighted Unit Values*, vol. 1, pp. 25–27, 29–30, 32–34, 39, 42.
a. Assumes 124 BMP fighting vehicles in 4 mechanized battalions, with 9 infantrymen per vehicle.
b. Average value for a given inventory of T54, T55, T62, T64, and T72 tanks.
c. Estimate.

Table A-11. Relative Value of Equipment in a Soviet Mechanized Division

Weapon category	Number of weapons	×	Weapon effectiveness index	×	Category weight (offensive)	=	Weighted value
Small arms	3,531[a]		1.00		1		3,531
Armored personnel carriers							
BRDM-1	153		0.68		13		1,353
BTR60PB	210		1.07		13		2,921
Tanks	215		1.02[b]		64		14,035
Armored reconnaissance vehicles							
PT76	22		0.75		36		594
BRDM/Sagger	27		0.70		36		680
Antitank weapons							
BMP	112		0.89		27		2,691
Sagger	36		0.50		27		486
T12	18		0.52		27		253
SPG9	12		0.21		27		68
Artillery							
M1975	18		0.44[c]		72		570
M1974	6		0.44[c]		72		190
D30	72		0.40		72		2,074
BM21	18		0.54		72		700
Mortars							
M1943	54		1.01		37		2,018
Weighted unit value	...		...		...		32,164
Armored division equivalent	...		...		...		0.68

Sources: U.S. Department of the Army, *Handbook on Soviet Ground Forces*, FM30-40 (U.S. Government Printing Office, 1975), app. A, p. A-3. IISS, *Military Balance, 1978–1979*, pp. 102–03; *1980–1981*, p. 10. U.S. Army, *Weapon Effectiveness Indices/Weighted Unit Values*, vol. 1, pp. 25–27, 29–30, 32–34, 39, 42.

a. Assumes 103 BMP fighting vehicles in mechanized battalions and companies, with 10 infantrymen per vehicle, and 186 BTR60 personnel carriers in mechanized battalions with 14 infantrymen per carrier.
b. Average value for a given force of T54, T55, T62, T64, and T72 tanks.
c. Estimate.

Table A-12. **Relative Value of Equipment in an Eastern European Armored Division**

Equipment category	Number of weapons	×	Weapon effectiveness index	×	Category weight (offensive)	=	Weighted value
Small arms	1,116[a]		1.00		1		1,116
Armored personnel carriers							
OT65	136		0.78		13		1,379
Tanks							
T55	325		0.89		64		18,512
Armored reconnaissance vehicles							
PT76	10		0.75		36		270
BRDM/Sagger	9		0.70		36		227
Antitank weapons							
BMP	132		0.89		27		3,172
Sagger	12		0.50		27		162
SPG9	9		0.21		27		51
Artillery							
D30	54		0.40		72		1,555
RM70	24		0.55[b]		72		950
Mortars							
M1943	18		1.01		37		673
Weighted unit value	...		...		...		28,067
Armored division equivalent	...		...		...		0.59

Sources: U.S. Department of the Army, *Handbook on Soviet Ground Forces*, app. A. IISS, *Military Balance, 1980–1981*, pp. 15–17; *1978–1979*, pp. 102–03. U.S. Army, *Weapon Effectiveness Indices/Weighted Unit Values*, vol. 1, pp. 25–27, 29–30, 32–34, 39, 42.

a. Assumed same as for Soviet division.
b. Estimate.

Table A-13. Relative Value of Equipment in an Eastern European Mechanized Division

Equipment category	Number of weapons	×	Weapon effectiveness index	×	Category weight (offensive)	=	Weighted value
Small arms	3,531[a]		1.00		1		3,531
Armored personnel carriers							
BTR60PB	322		1.07		13		4,479
OT65	165		0.78		13		1,673
Tanks							
T55	266		0.89		64		15,151
Armored reconnaissance vehicles							
PT76	10		0.75		36		270
BRDM/Sagger	27		0.70		36		680
Antitank weapons							
Sagger	36		0.50		27		486
T12	18		0.52		27		253
SPG9	12		0.21		27		68
Artillery							
D30	36		0.40		72		1,037
D20	12		0.40		72		346
RM70	24		0.55[b]		72		950
Mortars							
M1943	54		1.01		37		2,018
Weighted unit value	...		...		...		30,942
Armored division equivalent	...		...		...		0.65

Sources: Same as for table A-12.
a. Assumed same as for Soviet counterpart.
b. Estimate.

Table A-14. **Relative Value of Equipment in Warsaw Pact Units Held at Front or Army Level**

Unit and weapon category	Number of weapons	×	Weapon effectiveness index	×	Category weight (offensive)	=	Weighted value
Artillery division							
Artillery							
M55	18		0.46		72		596
BM21	36		0.54		72		1,400
M46	54		0.46		72		1,788
D1	54		0.39		72		1,516
Antitank weapons							
T12	18		0.52		27		253
WUV	...		...		...		5,553
ADE	...		...		...		0.12
Artillery brigade							
Artillery							
D1	18		0.39		72		505
M46	36		0.46		72		1,192
Antitank weapons							
T12	18		0.52		27		253
WUV	...		...		...		1,950
ADE	...		...		...		0.04
Independent tank battalion							
Tanks							
T55	40		0.89		64		2,278
WUV	...		...		...		2,278
ADE	...		...		...		0.05

Sources: U.S. Department of the Army, Office of the Assistant Chief of Staff for Intelligence, *Military Operations of the Soviet Army*, USAITAD report 14-U-76 (Department of the Army, 1976), pp. 79–81, 90–92; Friedrich Wiener and William J. Lewis, *The Warsaw Pact Armies* (Vienna: Carl Ueberreuter, 1977), pp. 64–67; U.S. Army, *Weapon Effectiveness Indices/Weighted Unit Values*, vol. 1, pp. 26, 29, 32–34, 42.

WUV Weighted unit value.
ADE Armored division equivalent.

APPENDIX B

Composition of Warsaw Pact Fronts

THIS APPENDIX describes the possible composition of four alternative offensives by Warsaw Pact forces. It provides estimates of their combat potential in terms of armored division equivalents as well as the number of men in major combat units.

A Two-Front Attack

The Group of Soviet Forces in Germany (GSFG) and the Soviet Central Group of Forces (CGF) in Czechoslovakia presumably would be the core of a two-front attack. Five Soviet armies come under GSFG command; and the GSFG is the only group of Soviet forces outside Russia to have peacetime control over an artillery division. Given GSFG's apparent preeminence, it is reasonable to assume that an artillery brigade and an independent tank battalion would be assigned to each army. Together, the 5 armies also control a total of 19 Soviet divisions.

This study also assumes that the East German Army would participate in any GSFG operation. In addition to 6 divisions, the East German Army could contribute 2 artillery brigades to GSFG's total as well as the suggested number of independent tank battalions.[1] A far more modest force, the CGF features only 5 Soviet divisions. These are reportedly organized into 2 armies, which suggests the availability of 2 artillery brigades.[2] Finally, it is assumed that no Czechoslovak combat units—

---

1. International Institute for Strategic Studies, *The Military Balance, 1980–1981* (London: IISS, 1980), p. 16. Assignment of the 2 antitank battalions to the 2 artillery regiments would form standard, Warsaw Pact artillery brigades. East Germany's tank inventory well exceeds the number needed to fill out divisions organized according to tables found in *Military Balance, 1978–1979*, p. 102.

2. Friedrich Wiener and William J. Lewis, *The Warsaw Pact Armies* (Vienna: Carl Ueberreuter, 1977), pp. 61, 64.

except, perhaps, for 1–2 artillery brigades—would participate in a two-front operation.

These contributions amount to 1 artillery division, 7 artillery brigades, 5 independent tank battalions, and 30 divisions (9 armored and 10 mechanized from the GSFG, 2 armored and 3 mechanized from the CGF, and 2 armored and 4 mechanized from the East German Army). This force would command about 24 armored division equivalents and 387,000 men in major combat units (manpower equivalent to 21 U.S. armored divisions).

A Three-Front Attack

The Soviet Northern Group of Forces (NGF) deployed in Poland, which currently consists of just 2 Soviet armored divisions, would presumably be included in a three-front attack. It is assumed here that the NGF would be augmented by 1 of the 2 artillery divisions reportedly stationed in the Baltic Military District and would also assume control of 14 divisions and 5 artillery brigades contributed by the Polish Army.[3] In addition, 10 divisions, 1 airborne regiment, and 1–2 artillery brigades from the Czechoslovak Army would be assigned to the CGF. Combined deployments might amount to 2 artillery divisions, 12 artillery brigades, at least 5 independent tank battalions, and 56⅓ divisions (9 armored and 10 mechanized from the GSFG; 4 armored and 3 mechanized from other Soviet groups; and 12 armored, 17 mechanized, and 1⅓ airborne divisions from Eastern European armies). Such a force would command about 40 armored division equivalents and 697,000 men in major combat units (about 38 divisions' worth of manpower). The Polish and Czechoslovak armies would contribute about 40 percent of this combat potential.

A Six-Front Attack

The Baltic, Belorussian, and Carpathian military districts would presumably be transformed into operational fronts to fight in a six-front attack. These three districts are said to contain 4 artillery divisions and 6 army headquarters, with the latter's presence suggesting the availability

---

3. Charles Kamps, Jr., "The Next War: Modern Conflict in Europe," *Strategy and Tactics*, no. 69 (July–August 1978), p. 25. Poland's amphibious assault division is excluded here on the assumption that it would be targeted against Danish islands.

of 6 artillery brigades.⁴ They also host some 33 divisions, most of which are maintained at category 2 or 3 levels of readiness. Combined deployments thus would include 5 artillery divisions, 18 artillery brigades, at least 5 independent tank battalions, and 89 divisions (9 armored and 10 mechanized from the GSFG; 4 armored and 3 mechanized from other forward Soviet groups; 12 armored, 17 mechanized, and 1⅓ airborne from Eastern European armies; and 14 armored, 16 mechanized, and 3 airborne from the western military districts). The combat potential of this force would amount to about 61 armored division equivalents and 1,080,000 men in major combat units (about 59 divisions' worth). The Polish and Czechoslovak contribution amounts to about 25 percent of these totals.

An Augmented Six-Front Attack

There is no telling which additional military districts would contribute forces for an augmented six-front attack or how many more forces would deploy. Although some assessments note that Warsaw Pact forces in Hungary could be used on the central front, these are usually assumed to be oriented toward NATO's southern flank (or Yugoslavia or Romania).⁵ While forces in the Leningrad military district could be used, it is thought that they are targeted against Scandinavia, while those in the Odessa, North Caucasus, and Transcaucasus districts are meant for southern Europe or the Persian Gulf.⁶ The Turkestan district presumably is heavily committed to supporting operations in Afghanistan. Reportedly, the 18 divisions in the Kiev and Moscow districts would provide a reserve for the central European theater, while the 6 or so in the Volga and Ural districts would act as a strategic reserve for all of Europe.⁷

  4. Kamps, "The Next War," p. 25–26.
  5. West Germany notes that forces in Hungary could be used against either central or southern Europe. West German Minister of Defense, *White Paper 1979: The Security of the Federal Republic of Germany and the Development of the Federal Armed Forces* (Federal Minister of Defense, 1979), p. 117. The IISS typically includes them in its totals for southern Europe; *Military Balance, 1980–1981*, p. 110. For at least the time being, the West has accepted this view in negotiations for mutual and balanced force reductions. Bulgarian and Romanian forces are also included in totals for southern Europe.
  6. R. Meller, "Europe's New Generation of Combat Aircraft: Part I: The Increasing Threat," *International Defense Review*, vol. 8, no. 2 (1975), pp. 177–82.
  7. Ibid.

Additional forces could also be drawn from districts along the Sino-Soviet border, the Central Asian being the closest. It appears, however, that many divisions in the Soviet interior are short of equipment, particularly armored fighting vehicles, trucks, and certain types of artillery.[8] Yet some of these units would need to be deployed to meet the division totals mentioned in some assessments. A major Defense Department study done during the early 1970s concluded that the largest augmented attack NATO might face would contain 126–128 divisions, including some from the regions bordering NATO's northern and southern flanks, the Moscow and Kiev districts, and the Sino-Soviet border. Analysts reportedly regarded this threat as unlikely and extreme, however, "because it would put Russia in a purely defensive posture everywhere but in central Europe" and because "some reserves would also be used to keep the satellite countries in line."[9] While a Carter administration review estimated that over 130 divisions might ultimately be sent to the central front, a recent study by the Congressional Budget Office focused on a 120-division threat.[10]

Although augmented attacks of larger sizes and different origins are conceivable, it is assumed here—in light of apparent requirements for Soviet forces elsewhere and shortages of equipment—that only 120 maneuver divisions would be involved, albeit 120 fully equipped ones. It is assumed that 1 artillery division and 31 maneuver divisions would come from the Kiev, Moscow, Volga, Ural, and Central Asian military districts.[11] Combined deployments would include 6 artillery divisions,

---

8. The IISS typically implies that Soviet category 2 divisions may lack some types of equipment and that category 3 divisions—which are the norm in central Russia—may lack some fighting vehicles as well; *Military Balance, 1980–1981,* p. 11. Indeed, a comparison of tables of organization and equipment with equipment inventories indicates that while the Soviet Army has a reasonably complete supply of tanks and tube artillery, it suffers from about 15 percent shortfalls in multiple rocket launchers and in armored fighting vehicles other than tanks. Estimates based on ibid., p. 10; ibid., *1978–1979,* p. 102. Wiener and Lewis, *Warsaw Pact Armies,* p. 60, report that most mechanized units deep within the Soviet Union would substitute trucks for armored personnel carriers and that these trucks would have to be taken from the civil sector.

9. Michael Getler, *Washington Post,* June 7, 1973.

10. Richard Burt, *New York Times,* January 6, 1978; Congressional Budget Office, *U.S. Ground Forces: Design and Cost Alternatives for NATO and Non-NATO Contingencies,* prepared by Pat Hillier and Nora Slatkin (CBO, 1980), pp. 19–22.

11. The Kiev military district reportedly contains an artillery division; Kamps, "The Next War," p. 25. No additional artillery brigades are included here in light of reports of a lack of army-level support units within the Soviet Union. See Wiener and Lewis, *Warsaw Pact Armies,* p. 64.

18 artillery brigades, independent tank battalions, and 120 maneuver divisions (9 armored and 10 mechanized from the GSFG; 4 armored and 3 mechanized from other forward Soviet groups; 12 armored, 17 mechanized, and 1⅓ airborne from Eastern European armies; 14 armored, 16 mechanized, and 3 airborne from the western military districts; and 10 armored, 20 mechanized, and 1 airborne from the Soviet interior). Over half the divisions involved would be category 2 or 3. The combat potential of the force would amount to 81 armored division equivalents and 1,457,000 men (about 80 divisions' worth) in major combat units. Polish and Czechoslovak contributions would amount to about 20 percent of these totals.

APPENDIX C

Composition of NATO Forces

THE first NATO ground units available for use in central Europe will be the active forces stationed in West Germany. They possess about 19 armored division equivalents' (ADEs) worth of weaponry and, at full strength, would include about 383,000 men in major combat units.[1] These totals include French forces, which are not under NATO command. These forces are excluded from some assessments, such as those by John Collins of the Congressional Research Service, apparently on the assumption that French forces could not easily be reintegrated into the NATO command structure in wartime.[2] France has, however, continued to engage in joint exercises and planning with NATO since 1967.[3] Fischer maintains that the presence of French forces in West Germany "is a political and military fact, and it seems reasonable to take account of it."[4] Alain Enthoven, a former assistant secretary of defense, argues that a presumption of full Eastern European participation in any war should be balanced by including French forces on NATO's side.[5] Domestic politics have discouraged public moves by the French government that would indicate a reembracement of NATO. As far as the West German government is concerned, however, "France has never left any doubt that she would honor her commitments to the Alliance in the event of a military conflict."[6]

1. Figures are based on table 3-3 and on unit strengths provided in app. A.
2. *Congressional Record,* daily ed., August 5, 1977, p. S27597.
3. Leon Sloss, *NATO Reform: Prospects and Priorities,* Georgetown University, Center for Strategic and International Studies, Washington Papers, vol. 3, no. 3 (Sage, 1975), p. 20.
4. Robert Lucas Fischer, *Defending the Central Front: The Balance of Forces,* Adelphi Paper 127 (London: International Institute for Strategic Studies, 1976), p. 7.
5. Alain C. Enthoven, "U.S. Forces in Europe: How Many? Doing What?" *Foreign Affairs,* vol. 53 (April 1975), p. 517.
6. West German Minister of Defense, *White Paper 1979: The Security of the Federal*

Other Western European forces would contribute another 9 ADEs worth of weaponry and another 229,000 men in major combat units. A Danish division is included on the grounds that one is apparently earmarked to join West German forces in Schleswig-Holstein.[7] It also seems reasonable to include here an additional 2 corps and 9 divisions from France.[8] The combat brigades and regiments of West Germany's Territorial Army are included even though they are ignored in some assessments, such as those by Collins (perhaps because the Territorial Army would operate under national rather than NATO control and because past West German statements have emphasized its support and rear-area security functions).[9] Fischer and the IISS are among those who count the 6 brigades that have been part of the Territorial Army for the past several years, while West German statements indicate that these forces stand ready to assist in forward defense.[10] Analysts in the Congressional Budget Office note that its significant combat power provides another argument for including the Territorial Army in any assessment.[11] Those units from it listed in table 3-3 would contribute about 67,000 men and over 2 ADEs' worth of weaponry. Although the light home defense regiments are oriented toward rear areas, providing for those areas' security, Fischer notes, "is not necessarily an unimportant function" in light of Soviet doctrine and capabilities and the presence of NATO headquarters, weapon stockpiles, and so on.[12]

Republic of Germany and the Development of the Federal Armed Forces (Federal Minister of Defense, 1979), p. 118.

7. See General Sir John Sharp, "The Northern Flank," *Journal of the Royal United Services Institute for Defence Studies*, vol. 121 (December 1976), p. 14. West Germany north of the Elbe River is defined as part of NATO's central region in this study.

8. This study assumes that France's alpine division and its intervention forces (1 marine division and 1⅓ airborne divisions) would be withheld or otherwise unavailable, and that French reserve forces would be withheld for home defense. See International Institute for Strategic Studies, *The Military Balance, 1980–1981* (London: IISS, 1980), p. 112.

9. John M. Collins, *American and Soviet Military Trends Since the Cuban Missile Crisis* (Georgetown University, Center for Strategic and International Studies, 1978), p. 362. See also West German Minister of Defense, *White Paper 1973/74*, pp. 32, 35.

10. Fischer, *Defending the Central Front*, pp. 17–18; IISS, *Military Balance, 1980–1981*, p. 112; West German Minister of Defense, *White Paper 1975/1976*, p. 113.

11. Congressional Budget Office, *Assessing the NATO/Warsaw Pact Military Balance*, prepared by James Blaker and Andrew Hamilton (U.S. Government Printing Office, 1977), p. 16.

12. Fischer, *Defending the Central Front*, p. 19. See also West German Minister of Defense, *White Paper 1979*, pp. 154–56.

Possible U.S. reinforcements are divided into three categories. Forces for which equipment has been prepositioned in West Germany would contribute about 71,000 men in major combat units and weapons equivalent to about 4 armored divisions. Other active forces, when reserve round-out brigades are included, contain about 152,000 men in major combat units and weapons worth almost 8 ADEs. This excludes forces presumed earmarked for NATO's flanks, for an Asian contingency, or for special missions. If simultaneous contingencies arise in Southwest and Northeast Asia, however, this study assumes that units containing 71,000 men and weapons worth 3.4 ADEs (1 corps, and 1 airborne, 1 airmobile, and 2 infantry divisions) would be dropped from the list of forces available for deployment to Europe. Reserve component forces, excluding round-out brigades, would contribute another 246,000 men in major combat units and weapons equivalent to over 13 armored divisions. In table C-1, NATO's ground combat potential over time is given in terms of armored division equivalents.

Table C-1. NATO Strength in Armored Division Equivalents, at Selected Times after Mobilization Begins

Country	M-day	Days after mobilization begins											
		M+3	M+5	M+7	M+10	M+14	M+21	M+28	M+35	M+42	M+60	M+75	M+90
Belgium	0.1	0.5	1.0	1.5	1.5	1.5	1.5	1.5	1.5	1.5	1.5	1.5	1.5
Canada	...	0.2	0.2	0.2	0.2	0.2	0.2	0.2	0.2	0.2	0.2	0.2	0.2
Denmark	...	...	0.7	0.7	0.7	0.7	0.7	0.7	0.7	0.7	0.7	0.7	0.7
France	...	2.3	3.6	3.8	3.8	3.8	3.8	3.8	3.8	3.8	3.8	3.8	3.8
Great Britain	0.1	2.2	2.4	2.4	2.5	2.5	2.5	2.5	2.5	2.5	2.5	2.5	2.5
Netherlands	0.1	0.2	1.5	2.4	2.4	2.4	2.4	2.4	2.4	2.4	2.4	2.4	2.4
United States	0.8	6.2	6.2	8.1	11.0	11.4	12.1	12.7	13.8	15.2	18.6	21.4	24.2
West Germany	1.7	10.2	10.2	10.5	10.5	10.5	10.5	10.5	10.5	10.5	10.5	10.5	10.5
Total	2.8	21.8	25.8	29.6	32.6	33.0	33.7	34.3	35.4	36.8	40.2	43.0	45.8

Source: Table 3-4. Armored division equivalents include units held at corps level.

Index

Adelman, Kenneth, 73
AFCENT. *See* Allied Forces Central Europe
Afghanistan, 28
Air power, 9, 10, 62–64, 99–100, 102
Allied Forces Central Europe (AFCENT), 31, 33, 35, 37
Army, Department of, 41n, 61n
Army Reserve: call-up, 18; decline, 27; limited mobilization, 21; potential use in NATO, 28; strength, 30; structure, 4–5, 8, 22
Army, U.S.: active forces in Europe, 66–68, 75–79; combat capability, 79–81; earmarked for NATO, 27–28; expansion, 3, 5; increased mechanization, 26; personnel shortages, 61; reduction in personnel, 14; reserve affiliation, 84–85; Special Forces, 18; Strategic Army Corps, 15, 18, 19
Aspin, Les, 47n

Balance of forces, 55–58, 62–63, 64
Bartlett, Dewey F., 45, 86
Belgium, 52, 86, 89
Berkman, William R., 30n, 62n, 84n
Berlin crisis, 17
Berman, Robert P., 63n
Betts, Richard K., 40n, 55n, 72n, 92, 95
Bigelman, Paul A., 81n
Binkin, Martin, 22n, 59n, 83
Blaker, James, 38n, 63n
Bonds, Ray, 37n
Bradley, Omar N., 94
Braybrook, Roy M., 63n
Brown, Harold, 25n, 26n, 37, 38, 53, 62, 69, 82
Brzezinski, Zbigniew, 68
Burt, Richard, 27n, 29n, 43n, 78

Calleo, David P., 73, 76–77

Canby, Steven L., 34n, 35, 38, 41n, 60, 70, 79–80, 81, 88, 89, 90, 91, 92, 99, 100
Carlucci, Frank C., 98n
Carter administration, 26, 28, 29; deployments to Europe, 52n; NATO reserves, 88; prepositioned equipment, 68, 69, 71
Census Bureau, 85n
Central Army Group (CENTAG), 34
Central Group of Forces (CGF), 45
Cole, Hugh M., 36n
Conference on Security and Cooperation in Europe, 25, 95
Congressional Budget Office, 38, 47, 48n, 52n, 55n, 66, 67, 68, 71
Containment policy, 7
Czechoslovakia, 23, 24, 25, 45, 46

Defense, Department of, 15, 16, 21n, 23n, 53n, 55, 62, 68, 70, 71, 84
de Maiziere, Ulrich, 33n, 87, 94, 95, 96, 99, 100
de Montbrial, Thierry, 66n
Depuy, William E., 32n
Despres, John, 41n
Donnelly, C. N., 40n
Dupuy, T. N., 59n, 94
Dzirkals, Lilita, 41n

Eisenhower administration, 13–14, 15
Enthoven, Alain C., 17n, 20n
Evans, Rowland, 32n

Fialka, John J., 29n, 88n
Fischer, Robert Lucas, 40n, 43n, 47n, 49n, 59, 60, 61, 83
Force ratios, 38–39, 56
Force-to-space ratios, 36–37, 55
Ford administration, 25–26
Forward defense strategy, 32, 86–87
France, 86, 88

135

136   Defense of Central Europe

Fronts, 41
Futrell, Robert Frank, 10n

Gains, Mike, 52n
Gelb, Leslie H., 24n
Getler, Michael, 43n, 49n, 60n, 84n
Great Britain, 86
Greenfield, Kent Roberts, 5n
Ground forces, U.S.: buildup, 3, 6, 11, 13; contingency requirement, 35–36; for Europe, 17, 27–28; reduction, 6, 7, 14; in Vietnam, 20, 21
Group of Soviet Forces in Germany (GSFG), 45

Hahn, Walter F., 78n
Haig, Alexander M., 45
Halloran, Richard, 66n
Hamilton, Andrew, 38n, 63n
Hammond, Paul Y., 14n, 67n
Hamre, John J., 52n, 53n, 68n
Hart, B. H. Liddell, 36, 37, 94n
Hassner, Pierre, 78n
Hauser, William L., 73, 74
Head, Richard G., 39n
Heiman, Leo, 61n
Herspring, Dale R., 46n
Herzog, Chaim, 94n
Hillier, Pat, 38n, 66n
Horowitz, Dan, 49n
Howard, Michael, 93n, 97
Huntington, Samuel P., 6, 7, 12n
Hunt, Kenneth, 70, 72, 88, 89n, 90n, 91n, 93
Hyland, William, 72

Iklé, Fred, 78
International Institute for Strategic Studies, 30n, 43n, 61

Johnson administration, 20–23

Kaiser, Karl, 66n, 77n, 97n
Karber, Phillip A., 36n, 41n, 91
Kaufmann, William W., 19n, 29, 47n, 53n, 67–68, 69, 71, 79, 82, 85, 93n
Kennan, George F., 8, 78n
Kennedy administration, 16–20
Klose, Kevin, 47n
Komer, Robert, 72, 74, 79
Korean conflict, 10–13
Kuzmack, Arnold M., 24n

Lawrence, Richard D., 1n, 25n, 34n, 40n, 60n, 70, 71n
Lewis, William J., 43n, 60n, 61n

Limited mobilization, 11, 12, 18
Limited war, 11–12, 20–23
Lind, William S., 79n
Lord, Winston, 66n
Luttwak, Edward, 49n, 79n, 81

Mansfield, Mike, 24, 72, 73
Marine Corps, 3, 5, 18; earmarked for NATO, 27–28; required minimum force, 15
Marine Corps Reserve, 28n
Matloff, Maurice, 5n
Mendershausen, Horst, 49n, 91n, 92
Merritt, Jack N., 39n
Meyer, Edward C., 35n, 69n, 74n, 85
Middleton, Drew, 28n, 45n, 46n, 52n, 86n
Myers, Kenneth A., 72n

National Guard: active cadres, 83–84; call-up, 18; decline, 27; limited mobilization, 21; readiness, 12, 59–60; strength, 30; structure, 4–5, 8–9, 15, 22–23
NATO. *See* North Atlantic Treaty Organization
Naval force, U.S., 99–100, 102
Netherlands, 52, 86, 89, 90
Newhouse, John, 1n
NGF. *See* Northern Group of Forces
Nitze, Paul H., 82n
Nixon administration, 23–27
Nixon doctrine, 24
Nixon, Richard M., 20n, 23n
North Atlantic Treaty Organization (NATO), 9, 11, 24–25; air and naval requirements, 99–100, 102; air power, 63–64; central front, 31–35; contingency force requirements, 37, 38, 39–40; defense plans, 93–97; defensive positions, 58–59; deliberate reinforcements, 82–84; ground forces, 48–49, 52–53; logistical support, 61–62; mobilization lag, 55; mobilization posture, 56–57, 58; reserve readiness, 59–60; reserve units, 88–93, 103; U.S. contribution, 65–79
Northern Army Group (NORTHAG), 34
Northern Group of Forces (NGF), 45
Novak, Robert, 32n
NSC-*68*, 10, 11
Nuclear deterrence, 2, 89
Nunn, Sam, 45, 65, 86, 97–98, 100

Operational reserves, 37–38, 55
Osgood, Robert Endicott, 7n, 10n, 13n, 16
Owen, Henry, 24n

Palmer, Robert R., 5n

Index 137

Pechman, Joseph A., 47n, 67n
Pfaltzgraff, Robert L., Jr., 78n
Philipp, Udo, 35n
Poland, 45, 46
Polk, James H., 34n, 81n

Radford plan, 14
Record, Jeffrey, 1n, 25n, 34n, 41n, 43n, 60n, 70, 71n
Reserve forces, 3, 7, 9; Carter administration, 28–29; efficiency, 22; integration with active forces, 84–85; limited mobilization, 11–12, 18; readiness, 21, 67, 68; reorganization, 15, 19
Reserve Forces Act of *1955*, 15
Ries, Thomas, 87n
Rokke, Ervin J., 39n

Sabrosky, Alan Ned, 83
Savkin, V. Ye., 40n, 41n
Schilling, Warner R., 14n, 67n
Schlemmer, Benjamin F., 29n
Schlesinger, James R., 25n, 26n, 35–36, 38, 39, 59
Scotter, William, 91n
Sidorenko, A. A., 40n
Slatkin, Nora, 38n, 66n, 69n, 71n
Sloss, Leon, 87, 90, 91, 100
Smith, K. Wayne, 17n, 20n
Snyder, Glenn H., 14n, 67n
Soviet Union: invasion of Afghanistan, 28; invasion of Czechoslovakia, 23, 24, 25; nuclear capabilities, 16, 25, 64; offensive approach to warfare, 40
Specialization, military, 97–100, 102
Sprey, Pierre M., 39n
Starry, Donn A., 39n
Strike Command, 19, 26

Taylor, Maxwell D., 15n, 20n, 73, 75–76, 82
Thompson, W. Scott, 65n, 72n, 78n, 79n
Tillson, John C. F., 93, 94, 95, 96
Truman administration, 6, 7–8, 10
Turner, Stansfield, 74, 79
Tuttle, William G. P., Jr., 81n

U.S. role in NATO: active force structure, 66–68, 75–79, 103; air and naval requirements, 99–100, 102; combat capability, 79–81, 103; commitment to Western Europe defense, 1, 11, 21–22; deliberate reinforcement, 82–84; forward deployment of forces, 71–72, 73–74; ground reinforcements, 52–53; prepositioned equipment, 68–72, 82–83; Reforger exercises, 22, 69. *See also* Army, U.S.; Ground forces, U.S; Reserve forces

Vardamis, Alex A., 88
Vigor, P. H., 41n
Vinocur, John, 88n
Volgyes, Ivan, 46n
Vought, Donald B., 37n

Walker, Emmett H., Jr., 30n, 84n
Walker, Walton, 10n
Walsh, Edward, 32n
Warsaw Pact, 20; air power, 62–63; army readiness categories, 42–43, 60; attack goals, 40–41; command, control, and communications, 62; logistical support, 60–61; mobilization, 43–48
Warsaw Treaty of *1955*, 46
Watt, David, 66n
Weigley, Russell F., 3n, 5n, 6n, 12n, 18n, 21n, 81n
Weinberger, Caspar W., 66
West, Francis J., Jr., 72
West Germany: allied deployments, 86–87; border defensive zone, 93–95; expansion of army, 87–88; forward defense, 32; mobilization, 49; rearmament, 20; Reforger exercises, 22, 69; U.S. ground forces, 1, 11, 21–22
Whaley, Barton, 41n
White, William D., 63n
Wiener, Friedrich, 43n, 60n, 61n
Wiley, Bell I., 5n
Wilson, George C., 72n, 74n

Zakheim, Dov S., 67n
Zierdt, John G., Jr., 81n